The Yakimas

BIBLIOGRAPHICAL SERIES
*The Newberry Library Center
for the History of the American Indian*

General Editor
Francis Jennings

Assistant Editor
William R. Swagerty

The Center Is Supported by Grants from

The National Endowment for the Humanities
The Ford Foundation
The W. Clement and Jessie V. Stone Foundation
The Woods Charitable Fund, Inc.
Mr. Gaylord Donnelley
The Andrew W. Mellon Foundation
The Robert R. McCormick Charitable Trust
The John D. and Catherine T. McArthur Foundation

The Yakimas

A Critical Bibliography

HELEN H. SCHUSTER

Published for the Newberry Library

Indiana University Press

BLOOMINGTON

Manufactured in the United States of America

Library of Congress Cataloging in Publication Data

Schuster, Helen H.
The Yakimas: a critical bibliography.

(Bibliographical series / The Newberry Library Center for the History of the American Indian)
Includes index.
1. Yakima Indians—Bibliography. I. Title. II. Series: Bibliographical series (Newberry Library. Center for the History of the American Indian)
Z1210.Y3S38 [E99.Y2]   016.979'00497   81–48089
ISBN 0–253–36800–6 (pbk.)   AACR2
1 2 3 4 5 86 85 84 83 82

CONTENTS

RECOMMENDED WORKS

For the Beginner

[14]   Virginia Beavert, *The Way It Was: Anaku Iwacha, Yakima Indian Legends.*

[60]   Richard D. Daugherty, *The Yakima People.*

[67]   Cecil Dryden, *History of Washington.*

[101] H. Dean Guie, *Tribal Days of the Yakimas.*

[112] Maurice Helland, *They Knew Our Valley.*

[133] Ruth Kirk and Richard D. Daugherty, *Exploring Washington Archaeology.*

For a Basic Library Collection

[25]   William Compton Brown, *The Indian Side of the Story.*

[63]   Gerald R. Desmond, *Gambling among the Yakima.*

[95]   Earl T. Glauert and Merle H. Kunz, *Kittitas Frontiersmen.*

[102] H. Dean Guie, *Bugles in the Valley.*

[122] Melville Jacobs, *Northwest Sahaptin Texts, Part 1.*

[124] Melville Jacobs, *Northwest Sahaptin Texts, Part 2.*

[153] Lucullus V. McWhorter, *The Crime against the Yakimas.*

[156] Lucullus V. McWhorter, *Tragedy of Wahk-Shum.*

[186] Click Relander, *Drummers and Dreamers.*

[187] Click Relander, *Strangers on the Land.*

[196] Alexander Ross, *The Fur Hunters of the Far West.*

BIBLIOGRAPHICAL ESSAY

Introduction

The American Indians who constitute the Confederated Tribes and Bands of the Yakima Indian Nation represent many diverse but culturally related Sahaptian-speaking peoples now living on or near the Yakima Indian Reservation in south-central Washington. Aboriginally they ranged over a considerable territory. Subsistence and social activities extended their contacts north to Wenatchi territory, southwest to the Klikitats, and south to the great trading and fishing centers of the Wishrams and *skin* along the Columbia River. To the west they roamed the slopes of the Cascade range, and on the east they intermingled with the Columbia-Sinkiuses, the Wanapams around Priest Rapids, the Wauyukma-Palus, the Walla Wallas, the Umatillas, the Tenino-Wayampams, and other Sahaptian-speaking tribes along the Columbia River.

The etymology of the term *Yakima* is by no means clear. According to Lucullus V. McWhorter [156], an early settler in the area, the name Yakima was not a local term but was conferred on the people by the Spokanes or the Pend d'Oreilles (Salish neighbors) and is a modification of *Yah-áh-ka-ma*, which means "a growing family" or "a tribe expansion." Other suggestions have been made, such as "black bear," "runaway," "big belly," or "the pregnant ones."

There are numerous references to Yakimas in early nineteenth-century chronicles. In the journals of Lewis and Clark [140], Indians in the area were designated as *Cuts-sáh-nem* or *Shan-wap-poms*, and the river itself was called by the indigenous Sahaptin name *Tapteel* or *Tapteet* (also spelled *Tapteil*), meaning "narrow." According to John R. Swanton [242], the Indians were called *Tapteil-min*, or more commonly, *Wap-tail-min*, their own name for "narrow river people," referring to the narrows in the Yakima River at Union Gap, where a large village was formerly situated. Swanton [242] also lists the "people of the gap" as *Pa'ʔkiut'lema*, another local name. The Upper Yakima, or Kittitas, were called locally *Pšwánwapam*. In his journal entries for 1814, Alexander Ross [195] a fur trader, termed the people and their valley *Eyakema*. Ross Cox [48], a fur company clerk, recorded the name *Yackamans* that same year. The Reverend Samuel Parker [177] spoke of *Yookoomans* in his journal entries of 1835–36, and Horatio Hale [106], with the United States Exploring Expedition of 1838–42, refers to *Yakemas*. In the Treaty of 1855 the name is inscribed as *Yakama*. Lyman [146] suggested that *Tapteel* or *Tapteet* was the original name and that Yakima is of fairly recent origin, though in use when the first Whites arrived in the Yakima Valley.

The traditional country of the Yakima is along the western border of the Great Columbia Plateau in the lee of the Cascade range. The ancestors of the Yakima lived principally along the Yakima River and its tributaries in territory rising in the Wenatchee Mountains on the north to the Simcoe Mountains and Horse

Heaven Hills on the south, and from the summit of the Cascades on the west to the territories of tribes along the Columbia River on the east. Yakima villages were also scattered along the lower Yakima River to its confluence with the Columbia River near present-day Richland, Washington. The country is broken by the Yakima Folds, a succession of long, narrow, fingerlike ridges extending eastward from the timbered slopes of the Cascades, continuing down through rangelands and ranches into the sagebrush plains. The Yakima River bisects most of the Yakima Folds, and the Columbia River to the east carves an even more rugged course through basaltic reefs and escarpments of the Frenchman Hills at Vantage, the Saddle Mountains between Wanapam and Priest Rapids, and a 1,500-foot gap at the Wallula Gateway. From here it makes its great bend below the confluence of the Snake River south of the Horse Heaven uplift to flow westward toward the Pacific Ocean, becoming the south border of Yakima territory, along which were many Yakima fishing stations and the great trading centers and gathering places of the Plateau Indians.

The Plateau itself is a semiarid region of open, windswept country, rolling prairie, and flat plains or volcanic scablands, supporting a thin cover of sagebrush, greasewood, and various grasses. Willows, cottonwoods, and tall grasses trace the courses of perennial streams and rivers. Today rich farmlands and orchards define the valley of the Yakima River, nourished by an extensive system of irrigation canals.

A rich contrast to the Plateau is provided by the eastern face of the Cascades, with their forests and larger wildlife. The Yakima Indian forest covers approximately one-half million acres, almost one-third of the modern reservation. Ridges are covered with western hemlock, cedar, western larch, white pine, Englemann spruce, fir, and Ponderosa pine. At lower elevations, stands of Garry oak appear. One such stand surrounds the perennial springs known to the Yakima as *Múlmul*, formerly the location of a populous Indian village, and in 1856 chosen for the site of historic Fort Simcoe, where the first Yakima Indian Agency was located in 1859. At timberline, huckleberry bushes proliferate in forest "burns" and in second-growth timber; and at lower elevations, bitterroot, camas, wild carrots, and other roots are found. Wildlife includes deer, elk, bear, and a variety of smaller animals.

Unlike many reservations, the Yakima Indian Reservation is on land that was once a part of the tribe's traditional territory. Here seminomadic, loosely organized bands of independent peoples ranged over the land, gathering roots and berries and fishing and hunting to sustain themselves. They counted their wealth in horses after acquiring them in the European colonial era, and their basketry techniques ranked among the best in North America.

Because of the peripheral nature of this part of the Columbia Plateau, away from well-traveled avenues of early fur traders, exploratory expeditions, missionaries, and settlers, the Yakima people were among the last to be intruded upon by sustained White contacts. Most of the early exploration and fur trading were restricted to the Columbia River to the east and sout of them. The first White men to see the Yakimas were members of the Lewis and Clark expedition in 1805, sent up the Columbia River to the mouth of the Yakima River, where they found a village of people called Chimnapum, probably a mixed gathering of Palus, Walla Wallas, Nez Perces, and people later known as Yakimas. The *Journals* relate that the Indians "live in a State of comparitive [sic] happiness" are "of mild disposition and friendly dispossed [sic]." Men share the work burden with women and are "content with one wife." They also "respect the aged with veneration" [140].

Most of the first missionaries and settlers moved along the Oregon Trail, following the Snake River through Nez Perce country and down the Columbia to settle in the Willamette Valley in Oregon or on the Pacific Coast. It was not until 1841 that the first United States exploratory expedition passed through Yakima country; not until 1847 that the first mission was established in Yakima territory; and not until 1853 that the first wagon train of pioneers traveled up the Yakima River, crossing the Cascades at Naches Pass on their way to Puget Sound; and not until 1861 that the first White settler established his homestead in the Yakima Valley.

On 9 June 1855 the Yakima people were coerced into ceding 10,800,000 acres of territory and forced to settle on a reservation, set aside on a part of their ancient lands, to remain theirs "in perpetuity." The Treaty of 1855 that established the Yakima Indian Reservation also created a new political entity, "the Yakima Nation," a consolidation of fourteen separate but closely related tribes and bands and villages, represented today in a formal governmental body, the Yakima Tribal Council. This Tribal Council, formally established in 1944, is authorized to transact business on behalf of the tribe. There is also a General Council, comprising all enrolled Yakimas over eighteen years of age, who elect the Tribal Council.

Today, the Yakima Indian Reservation stretches from the Yakima River in the east to sacred "Pahto," or Mount Adams, and the summit of the Cascades on the west, a distance of about seventy miles. The northern boundary is set at the Ahtanum Ridge, south of the town of Yakima, and extends southward about thirty miles, covering an area of roughly 1,400,000 acres in Yakima and Klickitat counties. Rich farmlands and orchards with fruit, hops, mint, and so forth, cluster along the eastern border, sustained by an extensive network of irrigation ditches, fading into cattle ranches and rangelands to the west, where wild horse herds still roam, and ending in the forested resources along the foothills and eastern slopes of the Cascades. About 50 percent of the reservation is mountain range and timbered slopes, about 37 percent is open grazing, and about 13 percent consists of the rich, irrigated lands of the valley floor.

Of the total area of the reservation today, almost

20 percent is owned by non-Indians, who have ac-
quired the major portion of the rich cultivated lands in
the east. However, through foresight and doggedness,
the Yakimas have managed to retain about 1,120,000
acres of reservation land, held in individual allotments
and as tribally owned trust property. Many of the
Yakima people are poor by the economic standards of
the greater society, but they remain rich in cultural
heritage, in pride, in land, and in a sense of belonging.

Most of the people live in the eastern section of the
reservation. The total reservation population is about
27,000; approximately 80 percent are non-Indian. In
late 1980 the Yakima Indian Nation counted 6,646 enrolled members on its registration lists; approximately
5,000 live on or adjacent to the reservation.

An understanding of the traditional way of life
with its beliefs and values is necessary for a com-
prehension of Indian and non-Indian relationships in a
historic sense as well as for an appreciation of contemporary developments and relationships between the
Yakima people and their non-Indian neighbors who
share the Yakima Valley today.

In Yakima studies many official reports and archival records not only support the Indian position but
clearly point out the biases and ethnocentrisms that
have led to confusion, misunderstandings, and need-
less destruction of Indian peoples and their way of life.
The reports of Indian agents themselves are woefully
revealing of the inadequacies of government policy,
training, and directives, which led to withholding of

annuities, exploitation rather than protection of Indian "wards," hardships, and abuse of Indian rights, all in the name of "civilizing the savage." For the Yakimas this is particularly true for the periods of the treaty, the Yakima wars, early reservation, and allotment. There are military figures whose careers were jeopardized as the result of inept administration and misjudgment of the Indian issues, yet whose diaries, journals, and official reports clearly continue to exonerate the Indians from much of what was perceived by others as Indian responsibility for the hostilities. There are missionaries, government officials, and military figures whose letters and reports attempt to correct some of the injustice perpetuated in early settler and historian accounts, in which perceptions of the frontier situation equated "Indian" with other natural (and unnatural) obstacles to be overcome in their settlement of the West.

The material is there. Yet there have been no comprehensive publications on the Yakimas, a major Plateau group, either ethnographic or historical.

Prehistory

Archaeological evidence reveals that native Americans have lived in the Columbia Plateau for over twelve thousand years. The picture that emerges is one of almost continuous prehistoric occupation from the end of the Pleistocene to the arrival of the first White men

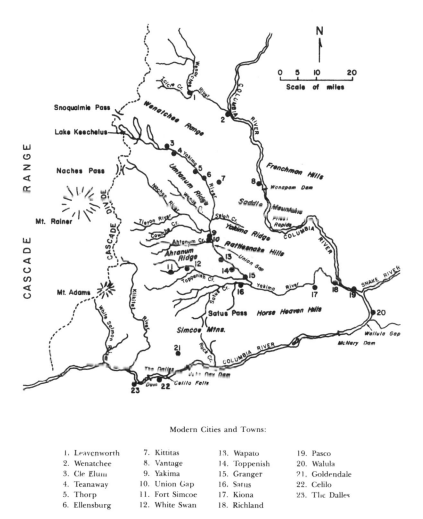

Modern Cities and Towns:

1. Leavenworth	7. Kittitas	13. Wapato	19. Pasco
2. Wenatchee	8. Vantage	14. Toppenish	20. Walula
3. Cle Elum	9. Yakima	15. Granger	21. Goldendale
4. Teanaway	10. Union Gap	16. Satus	22. Celilo
5. Thorp	11. Fort Simcoe	17. Kiona	23. The Dalles
6. Ellensburg	12. White Swan	18. Richland	

Map 1. Principal topographic features of aboriginal Yakima Indian Territory. Map by the author.

with the exploratory expedition of Lewis and Clark in 1805. Early cultures depended on hunting, fishing, and gathering wild plant foods. In general, cultural developments point to a greater similarity with the Great Basin and Northern Great Plains than with the Northwest Coast. Prehistoric habitation sites are found in caves and rock-shelters throughout the Yakima River drainage, and small, seasonally occupied campsites are scattered throughout the hinterlands. Large permanent villages existed along major watercourses from early prehistoric times into the historic period. Semisubterranean pithouse villages are known from sites spanning the last three thousand years, and one pithouse found on the lower Snake River has been dated to at least five thousand years ago.

About 3000 B.C., evidence of a basic shift in subsistence patterns occurs with the appearance of slab mortars and pestles, pointing to a growing dependence on wild plant foods and a more sedentary life-style. After 2500 B.C. a climatic cooling trend set in, and the plateau environment became much like that of today. Riverine settlements increased as fishing gained in importance. The presence of digging stick handles made from antlers and of fishing equipment such as grooved pebbles and sinkers reveals a well-developed reliance on fishing and on bulbs and roots. By late prehistoric times a subsistence economy based on fishing, gathering, and root digging, with less dependence on the hunt, was firmly established and continued as the dominant economic pattern into the historic period. Double

House Village, a late prehistoric site in Nez Perce country in Idaho, provides evidence of circular mat lodges and a parallel-sided community structure, prototypes of the historic tule mat lodges and longhouses used by the Yakimas and their neighbors.

Three recent syntheses of Plateau archaeology provide some of the best comprehensive summaries of regional traditions that have yet been written for those interested in the prehistory of this region. Roderick Sprague's chapter "The Pacific Northwest" [226] in James E. Fitting's edited volume *The Development of North American Archaeology* reviews the development of regional archaeology for the Plateau, providing details of the persons involved, the nature of their "digs," and the gradual development of interpretive understanding. His contribution is enhanced by an extensive bibliography. Melvin Aikens's chapter "Plateau" [1] in *Ancient Native Americans*, edited by Jesse Jennings, is a model of synthesis, bringing order to the morass of cultural sequences and patterns that have emerged from the rich data of recent archaeological investigations. Aikens traces prehistoric developments from earliest human occupation, beginning about 9500 B.C. (for sites at the Dalles, Wakemap Mound, and Wildcat Canyon on the middle Columbia River, Marmes Rock-Shelter and Windust Caves on the Lower Snake River, and Lind Coulee in east-central Washington southeast of Moses Lake) through five subsequent phases to the historic or Numipu period with its evidence of the horse, Plains Indian influences, and finally White trade goods.

Of particular interest are his findings [1] that "the subsistence-settlement pattern that dominated ethnographic Plateau culture had its beginnings at least as far back as the Cascade Phase," between seventy-five hundred and five thousand years ago, complete with the extensive use of salmon and root crops. Aikens's bibliography is also a first-rate resource.

Ruth Kirk and Richard D. Daugherty have published the third of these summaries, a superb text that can be enjoyed by layman and professional alike. In *Exploring Washington Archaeology* [133] the authors utilize their knowledge of cultural artifacts and activities to derive cultural interpretations for archaeological materials and features. Using this technique of "ethnographic analogy," they are able to flesh out both the people and their way of life—to make prehistoric cultures come alive. An added bonus is the collection of excellent photographs and illustrations of major and very recent sites.

One of the earliest continuously occupied sites, excavated by Luther S. Cressman and others [50], was situated at Five Mile Rapids at the start of the Long Narrows at the Dalles of the Columbia, a great trading center for the Yakima people This site, representing at least ten thousand years of culture history, was one of the most productive fisheries on the Plateau, where people harvested huge quantitites of salmon well before eight thousand years ago and where Plateau Indians still gathered to trade and gamble and fish, when the Lewis and Clark expedition descended the Columbia River in 1805 [140].

The Marmes Rock-Shelter, in southeastern Washington, fifty miles due east of the lower Yakima River, is an ancient site on the lower Palouse River. Its earliest occupation dates from about ten thousand to eleven thousand years ago, and it contained some of the earliest human remains in North America. A description of Marmes human fossil remains and information on radiocarbon dating of the site was presented by Fryxell [83]. David G. Rice [188] has written the latest report on this important find, which was excavated by Washington State University. The Lind Coulee Site in central Washington was discovered and reported by Daugherty [58] and is now generally thought to be more ancient than indicated by the original radiocarbon dates of 8,700 ±400 years ago. Recently renewed digging may confirm still earlier occupation. Quantities of bison bones were found in association with cultural materials, a good indication that the animals were hunted locally on the Plateau in prehistoric times Bison are also clearly drawn in pictographs in a cave on the Columbia River south of Wenatchee.

One of the first trained archaeologists to survey the Yakima Valley was Harlan I. Smith [219], who began his investigations shortly after the turn of the century. Smith identified numerous prehistoric villages, one at Union Gap near Parker, another not far from the Sunnyside Dam, and others below the mouth of Wenas Creek in the Selah district and in the Medicine Valley about a mile and a half west of the school. Among Smith's numerous articles is an interesting description of an unusually detailed antler carved in the form of a costumed figure from Tampico [218]. Smith's work was followed by that of Herbert W. Krieger [135], who first described the prehistoric pithouse village site on the Columbia River at Wahluke, near Vantage, with its decorated etched tools, shell pendants and beads, carved deer horn, wooden combs, gambling sticks of bone or horn, and many other artistically embellished artifacts.

In 1956 Claude N. Warren conducted the first important archaeological excavations in the Yakima region after Harlan Smith's work, completing an analysis of a stratified site on Wenas Creek for his master's thesis. This work was revised and later published [269] as a "tentative" synthesis of Plateau chronology and cultural affiliations. Warren's inventory of cultural materials includes many familiar ethnographic items such as coiled basketry fragments, stitched pieces of rush mats, gaming bones, remains of a decorated wooden bow, and shell ornaments, as well as dentalium shells and shell beads traded in from the coast. About twenty miles to the northeast of the Dalles a large site was excavated by Warren, Bryan, and Tuohy [270] that has been dated at seven thousand to eight thousand years ago.

Richard D. Daugherty's archaeological career is also closely linked to the Plateau. His important theoretical contributions began with the publication of his doctoral dissertation, *Early Man in the Columbian Intermontane Province* in 1956 [58]. His insights on the "Intermontane Western" and the "Old Cordilleran" traditions and relations between the Plateau, Great Basin, and Desert cultures still merit attention [57, 59]. Earl H. Swanson, Jr., who excavated at Vantage in 1953–54, also added a significant theoretical contribution to the growing literature in 1962, with his study *The Emergence of Plateau Culture* [239]. Charles M. Nelson's analysis and interpretation of the Sunset Creek Site near Vantage [167], built on developing theories of the early 1960s, is considered by some of his colleagues to be one of the most thorough analyses of Plateau culture history and related theory to be published.

From this same period, Robert B. Butler's controversial postulates on the "Old Cordilleran Culture" [33, 34] added to the growing body of theories as he continued in his role of devil's advocate. Less satisfying and equally controversial was the new framework for cultural developments in Columbia Plateau prehistory proposed by Browman and Munsell [23], which came in for its share of criticism, particularly by Swanson [240]

One of the best new syntheses to emerge in the 1970s was a proposed culture typology for the Lower Snake River region by Leonhardy and Rice [138], who had both participated in the spectacular finds at Marmes Rock-Shelter. Adding to the growing body of information was W. C. Smith's report [220] on the Umtanum Creek site in Kittitas, or Upper Yakima, country.

Carved and decorated artifacts of the middle Columbia River have been the focus of numerous studies.

A rich aesthetic tradition has been found in archaeological context from about fifteen hundred years ago to contact times. Emory Strong [235] presents a description of sites from the mouth of the Columbia upriver to the Wenatchi and Priest Rapids area, along with extensive quotations from early travelers' journals beginning with the Lewis and Clark expedition. Carved and incised stone, bone, and shell artifacts are illustrated, from prehistoric periods, along with early trade goods items of metal. Robert B. Butler [32] discussed "sophisticated art styles" that emerged in the Dalles-Deschutes area of the Columbia River between A.D. 1600 and 1800, expressed in novel forms of carved and decorated stone bowls, mortars and pestles, stone clubs with carved handles, incised slate ornaments, and antler and bone engravings. Claude N. Warren [269] reports on influences from this artistic florescence spreading up the Yakima Valley.

Petroglyphs and pictographs along the Columbia River and its tributaries have long held a fascination for prehistoric scholars. An early report on petroglyphs near the Dalles was written by W. D. Strong and W. E. Schenk [238]. Harvey T. Cain [35] provided further details on rock art along the Columbia River from Okanagon country down to the confluence of the Yakima and Columbia rivers. Emory Strong's work [235] is particularly useful for sites along the smooth basalt cliffs cut by the Columbia River from Vantage through the Priest Rapids area, and Butler [32] insightfully pointed to the influences on rock art in the

Map 2. Distribution of tribal groups and major linguistic boundaries, middle Columbia area of the Plateau, late eighteenth to early
nineteenth centuries. Mapy by the author after Jacobs [120, 123],
Maining [61], and Ray [182].

Dalles — Long Narrows area from southern Oregon and the Great Basin.

Early Influences, Contacts, and Change

The Yakimas can be characterized as one of the more isolated of the Sahaptian-speaking peoples of the Plateau. The Cascades to the west formed a physical barrier between them and the coastal groups; Salish and Sahaptian bands to the north, east, and south formed a buffer zone between the Yakimas and the Plains Indians east of the Rockies and their Shoshonean enemies to the south of the Columbian River. Extensive movement of peoples through the Plateau was confined largely to the Columbia River, which was peripheral to Yakima country. D. W. Meinig [161] assesses the influence of aboriginal environmental and social conditions on the character of Yakima life and offers some insightful evaluations of the effects of various factors for change.

The first major change in the older fishing-gathering-hunting way of life occurred with the introduction of the horse, probably about 1730. Francis Haines [105] has written the best account of the spread of horses to the Plains and Plateau area, and Frank G. Roe's *The Indian and the Horse* [194] is a standard summarization of articles and other "evidence" on the influence the acquisition of the horse had on Indian societies, including the Yakimas. Alexander Ross [195] reported that the Yakimas had horses for sale or trade in 1811, and his trip to the "beautiful Eyakema Valley" in 1814 to purchase horses has given us one of the most extensive and best descriptions of a large Yakima gathering and encampment in the early decades of the nineteenth century.

The animals thrived on the rich grasslands of Yakima country, and by 1874, as John C. Ewers notes in his comparative study [75], the Yakima people were fourth highest in the country in horse ownership. The report of the Yakima Agency for 1880 indicated that the Yakima horse herd had grown to over seventeen thousand. Ewers [75] also presents some limited but important information on the uses of the horse in Yakima culture.

The introduction of the horse brought about significant transformations in Yakima subsistence and social activities. A new standard for wealth and prestige was established, and intertribal relations were expanded. Yakima participation in buffalo hunting on the Plains east of the Rocky Mountains is recounted firsthand by Gibbs [92] and summarized as recollections in Guie [101]. Buffalo hunting frequently meant warring against Plains tribes as well as securing meat and hides, and it promoted the borrowing of a considerable number of items from Plains material culture, including new clothing styles, skin tepees and war bonnets. Both Gunther [103] and Griswold [100] should be consulted for information on the movement of borrowed Plains items from the Sioux, Bannocks, Kiowas,

Crows, and others. Griswold [99, 100] has also reconstructed trade patterns in aboriginal times between northern Plains and Columbia Plateau tribes. Anastasio [3] may also be consulted for Plains influences in the southern Plateau, but Ray's material [183] on Plateau-Plains cultural relations is too peripheral to the Yakimas to be of use.

Euramerican trade goods also filtered into the Plateau across mountain ranges from the East and the Pacific Coast, and up the Columbia River, long before actual firsthand contact with the Euramericans. When the Lewis and Clark expedition reached the Columbia Plateau in the fall of 1805, the party found many trade items already circulating among the Indians and being exchanged at the major trading center at the Dalles. Journal entries in volume 3 of the Thwaites edition of Lewis and Clark [140] and in volume 7 of Floyd Whitehouse's journal [274] are the earliest records of trade materials such as cloth, beads, and metal items. Alexander Ross [195] also documents the presence of guns in 1811 among the Nez Perces, Cayuses, and Walla Wallas, neighbors of the Yakimas, which they had obtained through trade.

Other significant changes among the Yakimas were brought about by the introduction of cattle and domestic crops several decades before the settlers moved into the Yakima Valley. George Gibbs [92] noted in his records for the McClellan party of 1853 that Chief Kamiakin had traded horses for cattle from the Hudson's Bay Company trading post at Fort Vancouver as early as 1840 and had brought the first cattle to the Yakima Valley. Shortly afterward, Owhi, another Yakima chief, imported cattle from Fort Nisqually on Puget Sound, according to recollections of Splawn [225] and Guie [101]. Gibbs [92] also recorded that the Yakima Indians had gardens in 1853 and that Kamiakin had already begun to use irrigation ditches to irrigate his crops.

Influences of a destructive nature also swept through the Plateau country as European-introduced diseases reached epidemic proportions among the Indian population. The first epidemics were felt most keenly along the Columbia River Valley, the main artery for indigenous travel, but they rapidly spread up its tributaries, including the Yakima River. The Lewis and Clark journals [140] contain observations on evidence of smallpox, suggesting that an epidemic had occurred thirty years before their arrival in 1805. Evidence of additional smallpox epidemics are reported by Teit [245], DuBois [68], Mooney [164], Wilkes [277], Gibbs [92], Splawn [225], and in the annual report of the Indian agent Robie [193]. Gibbs recorded that the Yakimas and Klikitats "suffered severely" in 1843 and again in 1852–53, adding that "the whole course of the Yakima [River] is lined with the vestiges of former villages now vacant" [92, p. 408].

In addition to smallpox, epidemics of measles, "intermittent fever," "ague," and "pestilence" swept through the Indians of the interior Plateau. The letters of Dr. John McLoughlin [150], written at Fort Vancouver in 1830 and 1831, described in detail the "fever" that was "carrying off three-quarters of the Indian population in this area." In studying McLoughlin's reports, Taylor and Hoaglin [244] suggested that the epidemic waves in 1830 through 1833 were "virus influenza." Cook [44] summarizes and discusses the known information on the epidemics of 1830–33 in Oregon Territory (which included Washington at that time). Useful but less detailed secondary sources are Anastasio [3] and Teit [245]. Teit also traced the evidence of the spread of measles throughout the interior Plateau in 1847, the same epidemic that precipitated the Whitman massacre and the subsequent Cayuse War.

In discussing aboriginal populations, both Mooney [164] and Anastasio [3] have attempted to assess population declines due to epidemics. Anastasio estimates that the Upper and Lower Yakima bands dropped from a population of seven thousand before 1805 (first contact with the Lewis and Clark expedition) to only two thousand in 1853 (McClellan's exploratory expedition through Yakima territory.)

Explorers, Fur Traders, Missionaries, and Other Early Travelers

The first exploratory expedition to enter the Columbia Plateau was the party headed by Meriwether Lewis and William Clark, whose original journal entries

covering the dates 11 October 1805 to 18 April 1806
represent the first significant general description of the
area utilized by Yakimas and related Indian tribes. Volumes 3–4 of Thwaites's eight-volume edition [140] of
the original journals covers these dates; volume 7 contains additional descriptions from the journal of Joseph
Whitehouse; and volume 8 is an important atlas.
Copies of the original maps drawn of this area accom-
pany the journal texts, and one of particular interest
shows the Tapteet (Yakima) River and other tributaries
of the Columbia.

Within a decade of the Lewis and Clark expedition,
the major fur trading companies were vying for control
of resources in the Plateau, utilizing the Columbia
River as their major artery. Some of the best descriptions of Indian life originate in the journals kept by
company employees. Although they frequently mis-
interpret what they are seeing, their journals contain a
wealth of contextual information, much of which has
never been fully explored as a rich ethnographic resource. The first trading post on the Columbia was established at the mouth of the river in 1811 by a group
of Pacific Fur Company employees, known as the "Astorians" after the owner of the post, John Jacob Astor.
This post was sold to the British North West Company
in the aftermath of the War of 1812, and Astoria became Fort George. In 1821 the North West Company
merged with the Hudson's Bay Company, settling a
civil war between the two companies, and in 1825 Fort
Vancouver was built about eighty-five miles upriver

from Fort George, becoming the new headquarters
and center for fur company activities in Oregon Territory, easily accessible to the Yakima Indians and their
neighbors.

The first records of the fur trade era pertaining to
the middle Columbia River are journal entries by
David Thompson [248] of the North West Company,
who became the first White man to descend the Columbia from its source to Astoria, a feat he accomplished during June and July 1811. Thompson described a Wenatchi fishery at Cabinet Rapids and a village of the "Shawpatin" or Sararpatin" nation (who
may have been Wanapams), as well as noting ethnographic details of dress, houses, language, and ceremonialism. Elliott Coues [47] first edited and published
the manuscript journals of Thompson as well as those
of Alexander Henry. A later publication of
Thompson's narrative of exploration was edited for the
Champlain Society by Joseph B. Tyrrell, and another
edition was produced by Richard Glover [248].
Thompson ascended the Columbia in August 1811
along with a party of Astorians, several of whom also
recorded detailed information about the Indian groups
they encountered. Among these were Alexander Ross
[195, 196], Ross Cox [48], and Gabriel Franchère [80],
all of whom joined the North West Company when Astoria was sold. Their varying accounts of a ceremony
led by a medicine doctor constitute an interesting comparative study. One of the best descriptions of an early
Yakima encampment was recorded by Alexander Ross

on his pioneering venture into the Yakima Valley to purchase horses in 1814. Ross's adventures [195] have been reprinted in a volume edited by Thwaites [249], and his narrative of fur hunting in the Far West [196] has been edited by Spaulding. Cox's narrative of his adventures on the Columbia River [48] has been edited by Stewart and Stewart [234]. Franchère's narrative [80], translated and edited by J. V. Huntington, has also been published by Thwaites [249].

Aside from these early sporadic contacts as fur trading parties passed along the Columbia River near Yakima territory, the Yakima people had little intercourse with Whites. As other company outposts were established, the Yakimas began to make periodic trips to the new trading establishments maintained by the Hudson's Bay Company at Fort Vancouver, Fort Walla Walla on the Columbia, and Nisqually House near the head of Puget Sound to acquire items of European manufacture newly introduced by the traders.

Letters, journals, and memoirs of Hudson's Bay Company employees are represented by Simpson [216], Work [281, 282], McLoughlin [150], and McDonald [149]. As governor of Hudson's Bay Company territory in America, George Simpson journeyed down the Columbia River in 1824–25, recording in his journals a wealth of information about the fur trade with the Indians. John Work was one of the company's chief traders, and between 1825 and 1832 he led expeditions to the Flatheads, the Blackfeet, and the Snake of southern Idaho as well as the tribes of eastern

Washington. His journal entries, often frustratingly short, meticulously record prices paid for furs as well as the condition of the Indians, their activities and beliefs, and so forth. Work's trip in 1828 along the Columbia between Fort Vancouver and the Spokane River is of particular value [282]. Dr. John McLoughlin, factor at Fort Vancouver, left numerous letters written between 1825 and 1838. Those edited by Barker for the years 1829–32 [150] contain many important observations on the Indians, including Yakimas, who came to the fort to trade. Howay, Lewis, and Meyers have edited the papers of Angus McDonald [149], chief trader in charge of Fort Colville, making available McDonald's descriptions of Plateau Indian customs, his impressions of Kamiakin, and comments on the War of 1858. Nathaniel J. Wyeth, a Yankee businessman, made several trips west between 1831 and 1836. Writing to Schoolcraft in 1848, Wyeth [285] expressed himself freely on the effects of epidemics and alcohol, on the inappropriateness of the treaty system, "as there is no resident Indian government with whom to treat," and on his sentiments against allotment and the division of the land. F. G. Young edited Wyeth's correspondence and journals [286], which have also been published in Thwaites's volume 21 [249]. A reprint of the journal of John K. Townsend, historian with Wyeth's second party, is also available in Thwaites's volume 21 [250].

Other early works that merit attention include George Wilkes's reminiscences [277] of his trip down the Columbia River in 1832. In addition to his general description of the area and its inhabitants, Wilkes offers some interesting insights into the beginnings of wage labor for Indians working for the Hudson's Bay Company. A reprint of Wilkes's original account can be found in the *Washington Historical Quarterly*. B. L. E. Bonneville's early visit to the Northwest between 1832 and 1835 mainly covers his stay among the Nez Perces, but is important for descriptions of Indian religious ceremonial and village political roles and for his notations on the introduction of Christian ideas by Catholic missionaries and traders (in Irving [118]).

Among the best sources are the records of the United States Exploratory Expedition of 1838–42, commanded by Charles Wilkes [276], with references to Indian gardens, irrigation practices, and other descriptive data throughout the narrative journals. Of particular importance is the account of Lt. Robert E. Johnson's exploring party from the coast eastward to Fort Okanagon and Spokane House, the first American group to cross the Cascades through a mountain pass (Naches Pass) in May–July 1841. Johnson's report of the country east of the mountains (published in vol. 4 of Wilkes's 1845 account) describes his journey through Yakima country near Ellensburg, his meeting with Yakima chiefs Teias and Kamiakin, curing and food renewal ceremonies, and so forth. Horatio Hale [106], a member of the Johnson party, recorded some of the earliest tribal and linguistic boundaries as he mapped the area.

The artist Paul Kane accompanied several Hudson's Bay Company parties on two trips west in 1845 and again between 1846 and 1848. The details of his observations and comments on Indian life in his daily journal are enhanced by numerous sketches, paintings, and rare portraits of Columbia River Indians [127].

Missionaries first moved into Oregon Territory in 1834 when a group of Protestant ministers crossed the continent with Nathaniel Wyeth. The following year another party crossed the Rockies, including the Whitmans, who settled among the Cayuses, and Samuel Parker, whose numerous journals went through many editions as revised by the author between 1838 and 1846. The 1838 edition [177] contains many details of Indian life, some referring to the "Yookoomans" and their neighbors; all are colored by religious philosophy.

Two Catholic priests from the Oblate order, Father Blanchet and Father Demers, began missionary activity in the middle Columbian area of the Plateau in 1836. The first Christian mission among the Yakimas, a Catholic mission named Saint Rose, was established in October 1847 by two Oblate fathers, Pascal Ricard and E. C. Chirouse. Ricard's memoirs of the founding of this mission and his recollections of the Indians have been translated by Anne Bounds of Yakima, Washington, and a copy has been published in Glauert and Kunz's reader [94]. Father Chirouse, who had been left in charge of the mission, left the area during the winter of 1848 when the Cayuse War erupted after the Whitman massacre in the wake of a measles epidemic. Chirouse returned in the spring of 1849 accompanied by Fathers Marie Charles Pandosy, d'Herbomez, and

Blanchet, and Saint Joseph's mission at Ahtanum was established. Pandosy published the first grammar and dictionary of the Yakima language [176] and enjoyed excellent relations with the Indians, in particular with Kamiakin, who became a regular visitor to the mission, though he was never baptized. A description of the mission can be found in the work of Winthrop [279], who stopped there in 1853 on his way from the coast to the interior plateau. Saint Joseph's mission was sacked and burned in November 1855 by United States troops, and missionary endeavors among the Yakima Indians came to a halt until Father Louis Napoléon St. Onge took up work among the Yakimas in 1867 and produced an alphabet and the first catechism of Catholic prayers in the Yakima language [204]. In 1871 the Yakima Reservation was assigned to the Methodists under President Grant's "church" policy, and the Rev. J. H. Wilbur became both Indian agent and minister of the tribe. The influence of Catholicism continued off reservation, undertaken by the Jesuits. The best general history of the Catholic missions in Oregon Territory has been written by Father William Norbert Bischoff [15], who is also the outstanding historian of the Yakima war years. Denys Nelson [168] discusses the role of Oblate missionaries in founding missions among the Yakimas.

The first large wagon train of immigrants to pass through the Yakima Valley was headed by James Longmire. The party took a shortcut through Yakima country and over Naches Pass on its way to the coast in

1853. A manuscript by Longmire describing the arduous trip, published by the *Washington Historical Quarterly* [145], contains some recollections of the Indians along the Yakima River. David Longmire's account of this journey [144] presents a brief description of Chief Owhi's camp. Theodore Winthrop, a young adventurer from the East, also crossed the Cascades in 1853 and recorded his impressions as he was guided through Yakima territory by the son of a Yakima chief. His popular narrative [279] presents a colorful description of Kamiakin, whom he met at the Oblate mission on the Ahtanum. Although he writes with typical ethnocentric biases, the caustic tone of his literary style is relieved by his wit and humor.

The Treaty Period

The relative isolation the Yakimas had enjoyed was soon to change as contact with military and government agents accelerated during the first half of the 1850s and pressures mounted to negotiate treaties with the Indians for land cessions. In response to increasing encroachment by Whites, Plateau bands moved toward amalgamation and confederation of their forces. Yakima "tribal" leaders emerged: the brothers Owhi and Teias (uncles of Kamiakin) for the Upper Yakimas (Kittitas); and their nephews Kamiakin, Skloom, and Showaway, who were also brothers, for the Lower Yakimas. Little attention was paid by Whites to the growing Indian unrest.

A West Point graduate and rising young political figure, Isaac I. Stevens, arrived in Olympia in November 1853 to take over his duties in newly established Washington Territory. His policies, which were to have profound effect on the future of the Yakimas, were compounded by the conflict of interests and responsibilities inherent in his mutually incompatible appointments as "governor of the Territory," "superintendent of Indian affairs," and "chief of the Northern Pacific Railroad Survey."

As part of the railroad survey, a military party led by Capt. George B. McClellan was dispatched the summer of 1853 to conduct a preliminary survey for building a wagon road through Yakima country and over Naches Pass to Puget Sound. George Gibbs, ethnologist and historian, accompanied McClellan's party. He was sent by Stevens to explain their mission to the Indians and to secure permission to build the road, but also to assess the attitudes of the Indians toward land cessions and permanent removal to reservations, in anticipation of treaty negotiations. McClellan's personal and official daily records, from 20 May to 11 December 1853, are an indispensable primary resource for Yakima research and are available in his journal [147] as part of the McClellan papers in the Manuscript Division of the Library of Congress. Tucked in between survey information and reports on meetings with Kamiakin and Owhi and notations on the disposition of the Indians are numerous windfalls of ethnographic observation and insightful comments on Indian life east of the Cascades. The best critical discussion of McClellan's journal is presented by Overmeyer [170]. Glauert and Kunz [95] include a typescript of journal entries from 2 September through 20 September, a copy somewhat marred by inaccuracies. A transcription was also made from original journal entries by H. Schuster in 1975 and is on file at the Yakima Cultural Heritage Center as part of the library-museum holdings. Unfortunately only a summary of McClellan's detailed report was given to Stevens for his Northern Pacific Railroad report [148, 229]. McClellan's brevity has been attributed to the antagonism that existed between the two men.

The reports of George Gibbs to McClellan on the Indian tribes of Washington Territory, also published in the railroad survey, are lengthy, detailed, and equally valuable to scholarly research [92, 229]. Both McClellan and Gibbs advised Governor Stevens against pressing for land cessions, treaties, or the creation of reservations on the Plateau as incompatible with the Indians' life-style. In a letter to James G. Swan in 1857, Gibbs reiterated his views, criticizing Stevens's policies in view of "the unwillingness of the Indians to have their lands intruded on" and attributing the subsequent Yakima War of 1855–56 largely to the governor's treaties [93, pp. 426–28]. Obviously, Stevens did not heed (and probably did not want to hear) either Gibbs's or McClellan's recommendations.

Stevens's reports of explorations and surveys for the Northern Pacific Railroad route were published as a twelve-volume set between 1855 and 1861 [229].

Most of the materials concerning Yakima country are found in volume 1 [228]. In addition to the reports by Gibbs and McClellan, volume 1 contains the topographical report of Lt. J. K. Duncan. Volume 12, the final report, contains significant information on McClellan's route, the status of Palus as "Yakimas," and other pertinent facts [232, book 1]. The railroad survey also includes copies of sketches by artists Gustav Sohon and John Mix Stanley. Those made by Sohon at the treaty council are of particular significance. An early critical review and analysis of the Northern Pacific Railroad reports was published by Russell [202].

Special Indian Agent A. J. Bolon also visited the Yakimas and other interior tribes in his district at this time. In his annual report for 1854, Bolon wrote of meeting with various "chiefs" of the area, including Showaway and Skloom of the Lower Yakimas, and convening a council of 220 Indians, led by Owhi and Teias, in Upper Yakima country. Kamiakin was absent from these meetings (see United States Dept. of Interior, Records of the Washington Superintendency [254]). Bolon's death the following year at the hands of hostile Indians was a principal catalyst in provoking war.

Any responsive, friendly attitude of the Indians toward the government agents changed abruptly when it became patently clear that Governor Stevens was bent on acquiring undisputed title to Indian lands. In spite of attempts by the Indians to organize resistance, Stevens unrelentingly pushed his negotiations for a series of treaties involving land cessions and reservations. Indians were to be compensated by payment of cash and goods, taught to farm, given a "White" education, Christianized, and ultimately "civilized." Reservations were represented to the Indians as assurance of exclusive rights to a bounded territory. In fact, reservations served to segregate Indians, sever their traditional ties, impede their access to subsistence resources, and confine them to an area where they were less likely to interfere with trespass or settlement. Coan [42] has analyzed the interaction between policies regarding Indian treaties and reservations, Indian unrest in the critical years 1853–55, the dissatisfaction of the Yakimas with their treaty, and other causes of war.

Isaac I. Stevens has remained a controversial figure, and a great deal of historical research has been devoted to justifying or condemning his actions. A collection of Stevens's letters, largely covering correspondence for 1857 and 1858 and housed in the University of Washington Library, has been published in the *Pacific Northwest Quarterly* [233].

A definitive, and supportive, view of the life of Isaac I. Stevens was written by his son, Hazard Stevens [227], who accompanied his father on many of his expeditions and treaty councils. His two-volume work stood largely unchallenged until Kent D. Richards, professor of history at Central Washington State College, undertook a special study of Stevens before writing another biography. Richards's initial article [189] is a brief and fairly neutral assessment of Stevens's role in the military conflicts in Washington Territory. His subsequent biography of Stevens [190] provides an objective counterbalance to Hazard Stevens's more limited interpretation of his father's career. As a nonpartisan, well-documented critique, Richards's biography humanizes Stevens by showing his frailties and the political ambitions that affected his policies, yet it also points to his strengths. About half the text pertains to Stevens's actions and policies that critically affected the Yakimas. Richards is also less critical of McClellan than is Overmeyer, justifying many of McClellan's actions during the 1853 expedition in Yakima country that have been criticized by others.

Early in 1855 Stevens sent James Doty, secretary of his treaty commission, as a special envoy to notify the Indians of the interior Plateau of a grand treaty council that would be convened the end of May in the Walla Walla Valley, site of ancient Indian council grounds. Doty's "Journal of Operations," dated from 20 January 1855 to 4 January 1856, covers this mission, the treaty council, Stevens's subsequent journey east of the Rockies to treat with the Blackfeet and other tribes, and his return to Washington Territory in the midst of hostilities. The journal is part of the National Archives [66]. A typescript copy was prepared by W. S. Lewis and published by the Eastern Washington Historical Society in 1919. Copies of transcriptions are available at the Yakima Cultural Heritage Center and have been reprinted by Bill Scofield in the journal, *Northwest Legacy: Magazine of Local History* (Selah, Wash.), and in the *Yakima Nation Review*. A Nez Perce version of Doty's

"Journal of Operations" is also available in the work by Slickpoo and Walker [217].

The Yakima Indians, about one thousand strong, arrived at the treaty grounds on 28 May, led by Kamiakin, his uncle Owhi, and his younger brother Skloom, along with representatives from Walla Walla, Wenatchi, Palus, and Columbia River bands. A large group of Nez Perces was already there, along with smaller groups of Cayuses, Umatillas, Columbia-Sinkiuses, and other Plateau tribes. Formal talks began 30 May and continued through 11 June. The Yakima treaty was signed the evening of 9 June, according to Doty's "Journal of Operations," though details of the signing are not recorded in Doty's record of "Official Proceedings."

The original "Official Proceedings" of the treaty council of 1855 are also in the National Archives [65]. A typescript has been filed with the Yakima Indian Cultural Heritage Center. Unexplained discrepancies between Doty's "Journal" and his "Official Proceedings" remain to be resolved, especially the accounts of Kamiakin's statements of 9 June and the actual signing of the treaty that evening after adjournment of the daily session. Incidents of Indian resistance to the treaties are largely played down or absent.

Lawrence Kip also kept a journal of events [131] that, while more informal than Doty's, largely parallels the latter's account. Kip's journal was edited by Frederick G. Young and reissued in 1897 [292]. A few pages from the journal have been published by Glauert and

Kunz [94], and the entire journal has been reprinted by Scofield in the journal, *Northwest Legacy*.

Indian Agent Richard Lansdale's diary of the daily proceedings at the council is an important primary source housed at the Beinecke Library at Yale University. While less well known than Kip's or Doty's journals, it contains some keen observations of events not recorded by the others. In an entry of 15 June discussing the treaty council, Lansdale describes Stevens's behavior as "not only arbitrary . . . but a little tyrannical." Unfortunately there is yet no copy readily available.

Various interpreters at the treaty council, including Fathers Chirouse and Pandosy and Andrew D. Pambrun, have corroborated Lansdale's impressions in their own papers. Pambrun also participated in the war of 1855–56 and served as interpreter at the second treaty council in 1856. A typescript of his personal diary, which can be found at Whitman College in Walla Walla, attests to the unresolved animosity of Kamiakin toward Stevens's threats and unrelenting pressures to conclude the 1855 treaty. Pambrun's original manuscripts were recently edited by Edward J. Kowrach [175].

There is considerable uncertainty whether the Yakima treaty signatories understood what they were signing. McWhorter was told by some of the old witnesses to the treaty signing that they merely "touched a stick . . . to show friendship only" (see introduction to [156] by H. D. Guie).

Josephy's history of the Nez Perce Indians [126] presents some discerning assessments of tribal reaction to Stevens's proposals, revealing Stevens's lack of understanding of the nature of tribal leadership roles and band autonomy among Plateau Indians. Kamiakin's disaffection and the widespread discontent over the treaty are also discussed by Josephy, as well as by McWhorter [157] and by William C. Brown [25], two other useful sources from the Indian point of view.

A comparison of resources reflects greatly differing perceptions of the treaty council of 1855. The journals of Doty and Kip and Hazard Stevens's biography clearly represent the territorial government and settlers' position, and they are the basis for accounts of the treaty council in Bancroft [10], Victor [267], Curtis [56], and others. More recent reexamination of events, based on these and the less well known primary documents and on interviews with descendants of those involved, takes into consideration the tribal reaction to coercion and threat. This point of view is represented by works such as Brown and Josephy. Useful summaries of events from a more balanced perspective are presented by Meinig [161], Splawn [225], and Avery [7].

The Treaty of 1855 created a new political entity, the Consolidated Tribes and Bands of the Yakima Nation, and established a formal relationship between the Yakima people and the United States government. An unanticipated social effect was to bind together with a formal sense of tribal identity the former politically autonomous local bands. The treaty was the principal catalyst.

The text of the Yakima Treaty of 9 June 1855 appears in Kappler's *Indian Affairs: Laws and Treaties*, volume 2, pages 698- 702 [128]. The indexes of this and other Kappler volumes indicate the location of other laws pertaining to the Yakima Reservation, covering such issues as irrigation, railroad rights, the Wenatshapam fisheries, agricultural lands, water rights, allotments, per capita payments, land sales, town sites, prohibition of intoxicants, roads, appropriations, and other topics. Royce [198] should be consulted on Yakima land cessions, which included more than 10.8 million acres of territory in the Treaty of 1855, about one-third of the present state of Washington. Further land cessions were recorded on 28 November 1892 and on 15 August 1894, when the Yakimas were forced to sell the famous Wenatshapam fishery that had been carefully retained in 1855 treaty terms. The Yakimas were paid only $20,000 for this 23,040-acre tract of land, or about eighty-seven cents an acre. This became cases no. 161 and 162 in the Indian Claims Commission docket [256, 257].

In 1857 Stevens commissioned a map of eastern Washington [231], indicating the ceded portion of Yakima lands, the Yakima Valley, and the Yakima Reservation and including a tabular statement of Indian population of the area. An error in the location of Priest Rapids on the Columbia River should be noted when using this map. A copy of the map is available in Gates's work [90] between pages 22 and 23.

The Yakima War: 1855–56

At the conclusion of the Walla Walla council, Governor Stevens and a small party left for Fort Benton, east of the Rockies, to treat with the Blackfeet and other tribes there.

Within a month, and four years before ratification of the Yakima treaty was to take place, advertisements by Stevens appeared in the territorial papers (*Puget Sound Courier* [180]) that the ceded lands of the interior Plateau were open to settlement. The land rush was on, even over farms still worked by Indians, to which settlers had no title. This latest deprivation added to a growing resentment by Indians of the flood of immigrants moving westward and trespassing on their lands. With the discovery of gold in newly opened Indian lands in the vicinity of Fort Colville in northeastern Washington, announcements were also carried by the *Puget Sound Courier* [180], and tensions mounted as bands of prospectors began crossing Yakima territory from the coast to the new gold fields, in direct violation of treaty rights. During the summer of 1855 hostilities erupted when a group of Yakimas intercepted and killed a band of trespassing miners.

On 20 September 1855, Andrew J. Bolon, recently appointed Indian agent to the Yakimas, left his agency at the Dalles to investigate the killings. Warned by Showaway to leave Yakima country because the Indians were in a threatening mood, Bolon turned back. While traveling south through the Simcoe Mountains on the

Eel Trail, Bolon was apprehended by a band of Indians, including Showaway's son Mosheel, and was killed. Major Granville O. Haller was dispatched to Yakima country from the Dalles with 102 men and a howitzer on a punitive expedition to avenge Bolon's death, as a show of strength and to suppress any further Indian uprisings. On Toppenish Creek at the foot of the Eel Trail, Haller and his force were attacked and routed by an overwhelming number of Indians led by Kamiakin.

Accounts of events leading up to and including Bolon's death and Haller's rout by the Yakima warriors vary, but the most reliable firsthand accounts appear to be those by Haller himself [107, 108, 109] and by McWhorter [156]. Haller's defeat at the hands of the Yakimas placed his entire regular army career in jeopardy, yet he steadfastly continued to justify the hostile actions of the Indians in light of illegal trespass by settlers and miners, stealing of Indian property, and violation of Indian women. Haller's "Kamiarkin — In History" [108] is a war memoir and tribute to the Yakima leader; the original manuscript is part of the Bancroft Library collection, University of California, Berkeley. A typescript copy of this and other Haller manuscripts and his original diaries and journals can be found in the manuscript collection of the University of Washington Library. Haller's "The Indian War of 1855–6" [107] is another important firsthand chronicle of events written by Haller in the 1890s and based on his memorabilia. An article published by the Daily Guardian Office of New Jersey [109], also based on

Haller's journals, diaries, and other papers, is a brief but excellent summary of the events leading to the Yakima War. This latter source also contains a copy of a significant letter from Father Pandosy to Haller, written in defense of the Indian position.

McWhorter's "Tragedy of Wahk-Shum" [156] relates the eyewitness account of Su-el-lil, one of the Yakimas present when Bolon was killed.

In contrast to Haller's reports, the confident and somewhat arrogant attitude of the territorial governments toward the Indians is reflected in a letter by Joel Palmer, superintendent of Indian affairs in Oregon Territory, dated 3 October 1855 [174], in which he states, regarding the Bolon affair, "Haller can handle it!" Good summaries of eyewitness accounts and army records are presented in Splawn [225], by the Yakima Tribal Council [291] and by Lewis [141].

What had begun as a punitive expedition and a skirmish erupted into full-scale warfare. Several tribes, led by the Yakimas, banded together to drive the Whites out of their country. The Walla Wallas, led by Peu-peu-mox-mox, formed another alliance with the Palus, Umatillas, and Cayuses and began hostilities to the south and east of Yakima territory.

Major Gabriel J. Rains was sent into Yakima country to avenge Haller's defeat. Serving under his command was a young West Point graduate named Philip Sheridan. The army was joined in the field by the Oregon Mounted Volunteers, commanded by Col. James W. Nesmith. The soldiers pursued the Indians to

Union Gap (Two Buttes), where the hostile forces escaped across the river, taunting the military as they fled. The army then descended on the Catholic mission of Father Pandosy on the Ahtanum and looted and burned it on 14 November, claiming that the Oblate fathers had been supplying the Indians with ammunition. Highlighting these events was the bitter exchange of letters between Kamiakin and Rains.

To Kamiakin's credit at this juncture in the hostilities, he offered an olive branch to the American authorities. Father Pandosy wrote the letter for Kamiakin, dated 7 October 1855. The whereabouts of the original is unknown, but a copy has been preserved in the archives of the diocese of Seattle, and a translation from the French is filed in the Relander Collection in the Yakima Central Valley Library. A review of this period of unrest, the role of the Oblate missionaries, the causes of hostilities, and a discussion of Kamiakin's letter was written by Nelson [168].

Kamiakin's letter was found by Rains at the mission on 10 November. Rains's reply, written on 13 November, reflects his ill-tempered frustration, projected in unequivocal, boastful threats to bring the Yakima people to complete oblivion. Rains's letter is part of the papers of the secretary of war for 1857 [262]. Victor published a complete copy of the letter in her history of the Indian wars [267], an appropriate complement for the kind of "frontier mentality" that characterized her interpretations of history. Colonel Nesmith sought to justify the pillaging of the mission and other volunteer activities of questionable nature in his correspondence with George C. Curry, governor of Oregon. This letter, dated 13 November, as well as the historically significant message of Governor Curry to his supporters, dated 17 December, is part of the correspondence and official records of hostilities from October through December 1855, published for circulation among the citizens of Oregon Territory [54, 169]. A copy of Nesmith's letter has been reprinted in the anthology by Glauert and Kunz [95].

Some of the regular army came to the defense of the missionaries. The aggressive pursuit of the "hostiles" by Rains's forces and the Oregon Mounted Volunteers was effectively criticized by Haller [109], who maintained that the Oblates were innocent of collaboration. Lieutenant Sheridan was equally critical of Rains's actions and exonerated Pandosy. His important firsthand accounts of the skirmish at Union Gap and the looting of the mission are part of his personal memoirs [215, vol. 1].

The territorial volunteers next descended on the Walla Walla Valley to the south, pillaging the countryside for supplies and food, sacking French–Canadian farmers and friendly Indians. The Indians suffered their first crushing blow when Peu-peu-mox-mox was taken into custody near Fort Walla Walla and was killed on 7 December while being held hostage. Parts of his mutilated body were taken for souvenirs. The Indians scattered for the winter, and warfare temporarily ceased. J. W. Reese has summarized the material on the activities of the Oregon

Mounted Volunteers during the winter of 1855–56 [185]. This article is also a convenient source for Cram's map of Yakima country during this time. The best eyewitness account can be found in the diary of Plympton J. Kelly [129], and two general articles worth noting are by Elliott [72] and Santee [205]. Sheller [214] attributes the killing to Nathan Olney, an allegation that still needs investigation. Some of the significant correspondence and reports from this general period of hostilities are collected in Furste's *Message of the Governor of Washington Territory* [272].

On his return from east of the Rockies, Stevens prepared an extended report outlining his entire treaty tour of 1855, presenting his version of the Walla Walla treaty council and post–treaty events, including his return from Fort Benton to the Walla Walla Valley, where the Oregon Volunteers were on the alert against warring Indians. Stevens dwelt on the hostility of the Indians, in particular that of Kamiakin. This highly significant report, written to George W. Manypenny, Commissioner of Indian Affairs, on 22 December 1855, was published as part of the Records of the Office of Indian Affairs [230]. It is also included in the report of the Commissioner of Indian Affairs, titled "Indian Disturbances in Oregon and Washington" [253] and in the report of the Secretary of War, titled "Indian Hostilities in Oregon and Washington" [259]. This latter report also contains the correspondence of Rains, Wool, Cram, Palmer, and other significant figures.

The famous controversy between Governor Stevens and Gen. John E. Wool, in charge of the Department of the Pacific, became public with Stevens's attack on Wool for refusing to assign troops to escort the governor through hostile territory on his return from the Blackfeet treaty council at Fort Benton. Issues also emerged over the conduct of the Yakima campaign, actions of the volunteers, and antagonisms between the regular army and the territorial volunteers. Wool advocated a return to a "policing" policy rather than pursuit of aggressive warfare—to regulate and protect Indian country while maintaining peace and security until the treaties were ratified. General of the Army Winfield Scott and Secretary of War Jefferson Davis both approved of Wool's policy. These principal issues of the day received extensive coverage in official correspondence and in congressional records. The Congressional Records of 1858 [263] contain the correspondence between Wool and Davis as well as letters that Wool pointed to as examples of antagonism of Whites toward Indians, such as that written by Rains on 29 January 1854, long before open hostilities erupted, but titled "Prelude to War." Cram's "Topographical Memoirs" [49], also provides an overview of the Stevens-Wool relations.

Letters and correspondence by Stevens, Wool, and others have been assembled in the Report of the Secretary of War, printed in 1856 and titled "Indian Disturbances in the Territories of Washington and Oregon" [261]. Some of these valuable documents have also been reprinted in Furste's publication [272], in Gates [91], and in the Records of the United States Army Command for 1856 and 1857 (see Congressional Records 1856, [258]; and 1857, [260]).

In the spring of 1856 fighting resumed with an Indian attack on the blockhouse at the Cascades, a critical position for the movement of troops and supplies up and down the Columbia River. The general uprisings spread. Firsthand accounts of the Cascade massacre are numerous. Among the best are the L. W. Coe letter in the manuscript collections of Yale University Library, the diary of Plympton J. Kelly [129], Lt. Philip Sheridan's memoirs [215], and articles written by Coon [45], Albert Thompson [247], who was one of the first settlers there, and F. M. Sebring [211], a youth living at the Cascades at the time of the attack.

Col. George Wright, in command of Northwest forces, stepped up his military campaign. Wright's official report [283] provides a comprehensive primary record of his Yakima campaign for the first half of 1856. This report, as well as other significant correspondence, is contained in the Records of the United States Army Command for 1857 (see Congressional Records, 1857, [260]) and is part of Bischoff's important summary of events [16].

Volunteers from the coast were sent to Yakima country as additional reinforcements, resistance was crushed, and a temporary peace was declared. A glimpse of events from the point of view of the militia is offered in the diaries of two brothers, Robert M. Painter [172] and William C. Painter [173], and that of Plympton J. Kelly [129].

It was an uneasy truce. In spite of hostilities, set-

tlement had continued in the Walla Walla Valley, provoking new Indian uprisings. Once again troops were
sent out, Maj. Robert S. Garnett's troops, to secure the
Yakima sector. Garnett began construction of Fort Simcoe in Yakima territory, giving the military effective
control of the Yakima Valley. The best account of the
history of Fort Simcoe is H. Dean Guie's *Bugles in the
Valley* [102], first published in 1956, followed by a revised edition in 1977. The book covers more than the
story of the building and occupation of the fort; it also
presents a thoroughly researched account of the principals involved in the Yakima wars from 1855 through
1858, continuing with their subsequent participation
on both sides in the Civil War—figures such as McClellan, Crook, Sheridan, Garnett, Stevens, Haller, Wright,
Wool, Archer, and Steptoe. Two other references are
useful sources: Travis's story of Fort Simcoe [251],
which is particularly good for the Indian Agency
period; and Culverwell's article, an excellent short review [53].

Governor Stevens dispatched Lt. Col. Benjamin F.
Shaw with a group of volunteers to the Grande Ronde
Valley in Oregon during the summer of 1856. The Mil-
ler papers at Yale University contain an important account of this expedition by Walter W. DeLacy. Shaw's
own version of his highly questioned expedition largely
against noncombatants is filed with the United States
Department of Interior, Records of the Washington
Superintendency of Indian Affairs in the National Archives (1854–56) [254]. Of particular importance are

Shaw's reports to Stevens dated 7 November and 20 December 1856. These and other significant correspondence on this "campaign" can also be found in Furste's publication [272] and in the Records of the Army Command for 1857 (see Congressional Records, 1957, serial set 876 [260]). The volunteers were disbanded after the summer of 1856.

By 10 September, regular troops under the command of Col. George Wright largely controlled the area east of the Cascades. Stevens called a second Walla Walla Valley council that same month, demanding unconditional surrender by the "hostiles," but Kamiakin, Owhi, and Qualchan refused to come in. Kamiakin fled to close relatives, the Palus. The manuscript of "Official Proceedings" of this second council, dated 11–17 September 1856, is housed under the Records of the Office of Indian Affairs, in the National Archives in Washington, D.C., as well as the cover letter-report from Stevens to Commissioner of Indian Affairs George W. Manypenny, dated 22 October 1856. Other correspondence related to the second Walla Walla council was published by Furste [272]. The typescript of Pambrun's manuscript at Whitman College covers Stevens's second as well as first Walla Walla council.

The major work on the Yakima Indian War of 1855–56 is the product of William N. Bischoff's dissertation, complete with detailed maps, pictures, and an exhaustive bibliography, which includes a critical essay on principal resources [18]. Bischoff has thoughtfully analyzed the extensive materials that pertain to this period, a task of considerable magnitude considering the bewildering amount that has been written, often housed in obscure archival repositories and too often representative of biases of the volunteer militia, or early settlers, or the regular army, or Indian-cause sympathizers. Publication of Bischoff's dissertation is expected in the near future.

A succinct summary of the Yakima campaign of 1855–56, also written by Bischoff, is less readily available but of equal merit [16]. This work also includes copies of the complete military reports and letters of Wright's campaign of 1856 and the map of Wright's expedition in Yakima country, drawn by Lyman Bissell. An article by Bischoff [19] discusses the problems he encountered while researching various materials on the Yakima Indian War.

Any research on this period of tumult must take into account the varying perceptions of events by primary sources, those principals who were involved from different sides of the conflict. For perceptions of the territorial governments, much of the significant material has been collected and bound under the title *Message of the Governor of Washington Territory* and accompanying documents [272], collated by Edward Furste, public printer of Washington Territory. This work has sometimes been mistitled "The Puyallup Wars." The 406 pages of documents and index are a prime source of information, containing correspondence, orders, reports, and documents, supplied to Furste by Governor Stevens and his officers from their files. The value of this collection would have been increased had this material been assembled chronologically. As it is, the reader must dig through the publication to sort out the sequence of various events and their influence on the course of the Yakima War. Nevertheless, it provides a rich resource and timesaver. Parts of the same correspondence and reports have also been reprinted by Peltier and Payette [178], Bischoff [17], William C. Brown [25], Gates [90], and Burns [31], and some can be found in serial set 822 [261] and serial set 859 [258] of the Congressional Records.

The diaries kept by the Oregon and Washington volunteers hold a wealth of personal experiences as well as firsthand observations on major events, from the fall of 1855 through the spring of 1856. Among the best are those by the Painter brothers [172, 173], Waman C. Hembree [113], who was serving with the volunteers in Yakima country when he was killed in April 1856, and especially the diary of Plympton J. Kelly. Kelly's diary, split into two notebooks, was brought together by William N. Bischoff from the Beinecke Library at Yale University and the Oregon Historical Society Library in Portland and published in 1976 [129]. An essay and annotations by Bischoff are included in this remarkable work, as well as maps, sketches, early photographs, and biographical sketches of 163 persons mentioned in the text—a model of historical research and presentation.

A wealth of information on the Indian wars from the point of view of the regular United States Army is contained in the Secretary of War's reports in the Congressional Records. Surprisingly, many are sympathetic to and supportive of the Indian position. The following are indispensable for Yakima research on the war of 1855–56: serial set 822 (1856) [261], serial set 858 (1856) [259], serial set 859 (1856) [258], serial set 876 (1857) [260], serial set 906 (1857) [262], serial set 956 (1858) [263], serial set 955 or 929 (see Browne [26]), and serial set 1014 (see Cram [49]). Events are summarized in serial set 955, "The Report of J. Ross Browne," special agent of the Treasury Department, dated 4 December 1857 and submitted to both the Secretary of the Interior and the Secretary of War, which included information regarding Indian councils in 1853, Yakima attitudes, especially those of Kamiakin, a review of the war of 1855–56, and also important correspondence from Fathers Pandosy and Brouillet. Another summary of events was prepared by Thomas J. Cram [49]. This report discussed the treaties, the cause of the war, and contained maps, surveys, and observations on the Indian operations during the Stevens-Wool controversy.

The journals and personal memoirs of regular army officers are also important to consider. For the Yakimas, those of Sheridan [215] and of Haller [107, 108, 109] are most significant.

Perceptions by trading post personnel or special agents constitute still another category of observers. For this period of Yakima history the recollections of Christina Williams [278], raised at Fort Colville, shed light on the "hopeless Indian situation." W. B. Gosnell, special agent to Washington Territory in 1856, placed the blame for the uprisings on Puget Sound on the Indians east of the Cascades, the Hudson's Bay Company, and the "foreigners" [98].

Perceptions of events by first settlers give still other interpretations, such as that of Albert Thompson [247] and Sebring [211]. Judge William Strong [237], who came to Oregon Territory in 1850 and became one of the first federal judges in Oregon, presents a position entirely "sympathetic to the Indian plight" in his discussion of the death of Agent Bolon, the subsequent war, and the actions of the Oregon Mounted Volunteers.

The reminiscences of aged Indian survivors of the Yakima uprisings are especially valuable for an understanding of the Indian point of view. These recollections have been collected and are presented by William Brown [25], McWhorter [156], Splawn [225], and Ballou [8].

The Yakima War: 1858

Not losing sight of the injustices that had provoked the Indians into war, General Wool tried to resecure the interior Plateau for the Indians, maintaining that it was a natural homeland for the Indians but unsuitable for White settlement. Wool closed the interior to White settlers in 1857 by military order, commanding all Whites to leave the area east of the Cascade Mountains and ordering Shaw out of Walla Walla country. Colonel Wright also came to the defense of the Indians, advising return of Indians' lands to meet their needs for fishing, hunting, and gathering grounds and stating that the treaty was "null and void" because the country was opened to settlement before the treaty was ratified. Significant reports can be found in serial set 876 [260] and in Cram [49].

Stevens served as governor of Washington Territory until 11 August 1857, when he resigned, having been elected to the office of territorial delegate to the Congress, where he served for two terms. 1857 was a year without disturbances, providing a lull between hostilities. But peace was short-lived. Further discoveries of gold were made in British Columbia, and prospectors once again traversed Indian territory to reach the mining sites from Oregon and Washington. Inevitably warfare broke out once more. David McLoughlin's gold-seeking party traveling from Walla Walla to the mine fields of the Fraser River was attacked as it crossed Indian territory. The unlawfulness of the volunteer militia added fuel to the hostilities.

Col. E. J. Steptoe was sent north from Fort Walla Walla to secure the area east of the Columbia River but was turned back by a combined force of Spokane, Coeur d'Alene, Palus, and Yakima Indians. In the wake of Steptoe's defeat, Major Garnett's forces were mobilized from Fort Simcoe against the Yakimas, and Colonel Wright attacked the Indian alliance near the Spokane River. The Indian War of 1858 was fully launched.

Wright's forces advanced against the northern Indian alliance. Decisive battles were fought at Four Lakes and on the Spokane Plains, and the Indians were in retreat. Wright's forces then captured and killed eight hundred Indian horses, as well as Indian cattle, and destroyed Indian grain, hay, and cached foods. The Indians found themselves unmounted, without necessary resources, and overpowered by superior weapon power. Hostilities finally ended on 17 September 1858. The Spokanes were forced to surrender on Wright's terms, followed by the Coeur d'Alenes. The Nez Perces, who had also joined the Indian alliance, signed a separate peace treaty. Owhi surrendered to Wright and was arrested and ordered to send for his son Qualchan. When Qualchan rode into the army camp he was seized and summarily hanged in the erroneous belief that he had been guilty of Bolon's death. This historical error and other errors of fact and interpretation have unfortunately been perpetuated in the works by Bancroft [10], Victor [267], Hazard Stevens [227], and Prosch [179], among others.

There appears to be greater consensus among eyewitnesses and later scholars as to just what occurred during the hostilities of 1858 than during those of 1855–56. Three useful sources on Steptoe's battle are Chadwick [36], Elliott [71], and Beall [13], who was the wagon train packmaster for both Steptoe's and Wright's expeditions.

There are many accounts of the Steptoe and Wright campaigns, but few accounts of Garnett's activities in Yakima country. An important firsthand recollection is provided by General George Crook [51], who served as a company commander under Garnett and whose autobiography, written between 1885 and 1890, includes a brief but valuable section on his two and a half months with Garnett in Yakima territory. In addition to details on the campaign, Crook relates how they captured and executed five murderers of the miners while on reconnaissance along the banks of the Wenatchee River. Crook also includes detailed descriptions of the countryside, Indian villages or camps, the "young braves," and the great quantities of salmon in the Columbia River. Reports and letters regarding Garnett's campaign are also published as part of the Report of the Secretary of War in 1859 [264].

The most important firsthand resource on the Steptoe and Wright expeditions is Wright's own military report to the Secretary of War, titled "Expedition against the Northern Indians" [284]. In addition to Wright's report, this same volume contains military reports by Steptoe, records of Garnett's campaign, and other significant documents pertaining to affairs in the Department of the Pacific during 1858 [264]. The "Topographical Memoir of Col. Wright's Campaign," prepared by Lt. John Mullan, also contains a wealth of primary material, as well as maps of the campaign and battlefield [165].

Two other eyewitness accounts that provide additional, and more personal, versions of the Steptoe-Wright, campaigns are those by Kip [132] and by Keyes [130]. Lt. Lawrence Kip's journal, which offers a useful chronicle of events, with some interesting sidelights, was published as a small book in 1859. Kip's entire account, though, of the imprisonment of Owhi, the hanging of Qualchan, and the death of Owhi is an almost exact copy of Capt. Erasmus D. Keyes's field journal of these events. Kip served as Keyes's adjutant, and much of what he wrote must be credited to Keyes.

Capt. Erasmus D. Keyes's own memoirs, published from his field journals in 1884, include a long chapter on his experiences in the western and eastern Washington Territory campaigns. As an extra bonus, Keyes has spiced his journals with personal descriptions of most key army officers involved in the 1856 and 1858 expeditions [130].

One of the best histories, particularly for the beginning student, was written by Benjamin F. Manring, an early historian [158]. This collector's item includes reproductions of many important letters, old photographs and military reports, which enhance his excellent overview of the 1858 Indian war.

Two other resources deserve notice, both of which focus on the role of the Jesuits in concluding peace treaties during the hostilities of 1858. Bischoff and Gates [20] present a capsule treatment on the Jesuits among the Coeur d'Alenes. Burns [30] reassesses some of the pioneer accounts compared with those of Father Joset, a key figure in the negotiations between Wright and the Indians, basing some of his interpretations on unpublished documents, a distinct contribution to research.

Most general histories of Indian affairs in Washington Territory during the tumultous years 1855 through

1858 are uneven, weighted in favor of the pioneers' point of view, and careless of their perpetuation of factual errors carried over from the eminent, and thus sacrosanct, works of Bancroft and his followers. A healthful corrective, "The Indian Side of the Story," is offered by Judge William Compton Brown [25], who lived much of his long life in eastern Washington in intimate contact with survivors and their descendants, Indian and White, of this significant period of Indian history. Aside from a few factual errors, Judge Brown has written a noteworthy account of these years, both historical and biographical, designed to fill in the record by revealing history as perceived by the original inhabitants of the territory. His work is especially valuable for its reexamination of the Stevens-Wool controversy, its inclusion of family histories and genealogies of Kamiakin and other Indian families, as well as copies and quotes from many key documents, such as Doty's journal, and substantial firsthand testimonies and anecdotal accounts of key figures.

Peltier and Payette [178] have also written a long history of the war period, from 1855 through 1858, which follows Brown's lead in supporting the right of the Indians to defend their homes and tribal lands but departs from his work in a strong defense of Governor Stevens's policies. The authors' most valuable contributions are the liberal quotations from unpublished sources and the Congressional Records.

The chapter on the Indian wars of 1855–58 by Cecil Dryden in his *History of Washington* [67] is also a

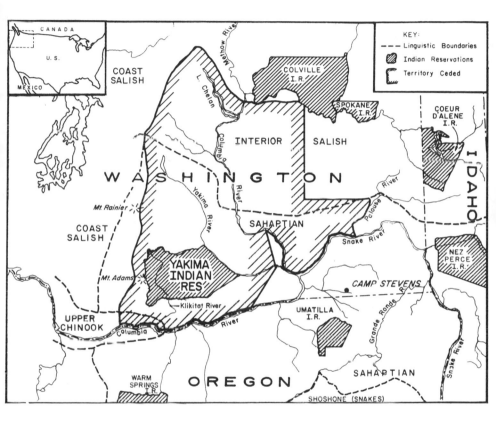

Map 3. The Treaty of 1855.

good overview and summary of these events. Dryden wrote his history as a high-school or college text. Dunn has also included a chapter on these Indian wars in his *Massacres of the Mountains* [69], an early popular work that stands up rather well for its time and is available in a 1963 reprint edition. Another early but good capsule report is presented by Prosch [179], also written in defense of the Indian position but still attributing Bolon's murder to Qualchan. Clark's military history [40] should also be consulted.

The Reservation Period and the Modern Yakima Nation

With the final defeat of the allied Indian forces, peace once again was restored to the Columbia Plateau. The Treaty of 1855 was finally ratified by Congress and signed into a proclamation by President James Buchanan on 18 April 1859, officially opening the interior Plateau to settlement. General Harney, who had succeeded General Clark in command of the Pacific Coast, authorized Reverend Pierre-Jean De Smet to effect a meeting with the chiefs of the hostile confederation. A major role in maintaining this peace is credited to Father De Smet and to Father Joset, another Jesuit, according to Robert I. Burns, in a carefully documented reassessment of the Indian wars of the Northwest [31]. De Smet's own account of approaching the chiefs, of their willingness to cooperate, and of their journey to Fort Walla Walla and then to Fort Vancouver to meet with General Harney is included in the four volumes of materials collected and edited by Chittenden and Richards on the life, letters, and travels of this prominent figure in missionary and political affairs [62]. Several critical letters by De Smet to Harney, relating to Kamiakin and his brother Skloom, telling of the "abject poverty" to which Kamiakin had been reduced and pleading Kamiakin's cause for a pardon, with Harney's replies, are also available in a facsimile reproduction of these documents under the title *New Indian Sketches* [61]. The report of the Secretary of War for 1859 in the Congressional Records [265] also contains copies of De Smet's and Harney's correspondence concerning the disposition of Kamiakin and his brother Skloom (serial set 1051), as well as other significant war records. Unfortunately, as Harney's correspondence reveals, and as a consequence of "officious interference," Kamiakin reassessed the situation, became alarmed, and returned to his refuge. Harney justifies Kamiakin's actions. Harney's letters also reveal that the Fort Simcoe military garrison had been withdrawn from the Yakima Reservation and that the fort had been turned over to the Department of Indian Affairs for the new location of the Yakima Indian Agency. Joset [30] also contributes a firsthand account of the postwar events of 1859.

Peace found the new Yakima Nation without experienced leadership as it began to adjust to reservation life. Kamiakin wandered through the northwest for some years, refusing to return to his reservation. In 1860 Agent Lansdale sought him out to try to persuade him to become head chief of the new Yakima Nation. But, though no longer hostile, Kamiakin refused, also rejecting any gifts from the Americans. Lansdale's report to the Commissioner of Indian Affairs for the year 1860 sympathetically portrays Kamiakin's position. Kamiakin finally settled at Rock Lake, a Palus community south of Spokane, where he lived in exile and poverty until he died about 1887. The most detailed accounts of Kamiakin's final years can be found in Splawn [225], Yakima Tribal Council [291], and William C. Brown [25].

The first Indian agent to take up residence at Fort Simcoe was Richard H. Lansdale. Many Indian agents served at the fort and at the agency at Toppenish when it was moved there in 1922 (where it is today). The most noted and profoundly effective on Indian life was the Reverend James H. Wilbur, Methodist circuit rider and pioneer in Oregon Territory since 1846–47. "Father Wilbur," as he was called by the Indians, served first as teacher, then as school superintendent of the reservation boarding school at the fort and was commissioned Indian agent by Lincoln in 1865. He served as Indian agent and Methodist missionary for almost twenty years, except for a brief period in 1870–71, until he retired in October 1883. Dr. Kuykendall was agency physician for a part of this time. Wilbur's annual reports to the commissioner of Indian affairs for this extensive and crucial period in Yakima history

(1860–83) are a mine of information on population estimates, ranching and farming developments on the reservation, housing, education at the boarding school, suggestions on how to "civilize" the "wild" Indians, subsistence activities, land surveys for allotments, and many other topics, in particular for the years 1865, 1868, 1875, 1880, and 1881. The report of Felix R. Brunot [27], Board of Indian Commissioners, to the Commissioner of Indian Affairs on a council held with the "Simco" (Yakima) Indians contains many significant statistics on the development of reservation resources. Important data and insights into this historic period can also be gleaned from the press copy letters of the "Wilbur Collection," housed at the Federal Archives and Records Center in Seattle. The correspondence of the agent who followed Wilbur is also part of this collection.

A detailed summary of the first hundred years of the reservation is presented in the centennial booklet *The Yakimas: Treaty Centennial, 1855–1955*, published by the Yakima Tribal Council [291]. Relander [187] also offers a useful overview, particularly for the "Wilbur years," and Splawn's reminiscences [225] are unique as personal recollections of an early settler. Some useful information on the Yakima Agency is presented by Masterson [160] in his article on the Washington Superintendency of Indian Affairs. Seymore [213] gives an overview of *Indian Agents of the Old Frontier.*

Significant events marked the changes that were taking place in the Yakima Valley. In 1861 the first

White family settled just northeast of the reservation, to be rapidly followed by other homesteaders now that the territory was officially opened. In 1866 a stage road was opened from the reservation over Satus Pass to Goldendale, and by 1875 a wagon road connected Yakima City with Goldendale. But the most rapid increases in White settlement and subsequent changes occurred when the Northern Pacific Railroad began operating along the Yakima River Valley in 1883. Meinig [161] contains a discussion and diagrammatic summary of railroad routes through the Yakima Reservation. In spite of this period of expansion in ranching and farming activities, most Yakimas continued to rely on the old hunting-fishing-gathering economy as their principal subsistence base. Desmond [63] compares subsistence commodities with livestock and agricultural products for the period 1860 to 1880 to illustrate this continuing reliance on a traditional pattern of life. Wilbur's annual report to the Commissioner of Indian Affairs for the year 1881 substantiates the slow rate of acculturation.

The bitter rivalry that developed between the Catholic and Methodist missions climaxed when President Grant "allotted" the Yakima Reservation to the Methodist church in 1867 at Reverend Wilbur's personal urging. Indian Agent Wilbur assumed a monopoly over spiritual guidance as well as government control, and the Catholics were banished to North Yakima City. Whitner [275] provides the best evaluation of Grant's "peace-church policy" on the

Yakima Reservation. An interesting comparison can be made of Father De Smet's attitude toward the Indians in his letter of protest to the Commissioner of Indian Affairs, dated 27 March 1871 [62], and Father Wilbur's tactics, submitted in his annual report of 1876 urging the use of force to compel the Indians to give up pagan ways, learn to cultivate the soil, cut their hair, send their children to school, and adopt "civilized" language, dress, houses, and way of life.

The rising tide of public criticism of government policy due to the inordinately high expenses of the Indian wars, and the naming of the Indian service as the most corrupt branch of government by a congressional committee, had led to Grant's decision to place the agencies under missionary control. But these same factors had also affected Indian attitudes, and Christian missionary efforts were rivaled on the Plateau by a revival of the Dreamer religion (discussed under "Religion"). The reports of Maj. J. W. MacMurray [151, 152], sent by Gen. N. A. Miles on a tour of inspection of Indians living along the Columbia River, offer the best description and evaluation of events on the Yakima Reservation as well as at Priest Rapids. MacMurray cites as principal causes of disaffection the impact of the railroad, resistance to Indians homesteading off the reservation (permitted with the passage of the Homestead Act of 1884), misapplication of funds, and the interference of the Indian agent (Milroy) with the domestic life of the Yakima people. In contrast, Milroy's criticism and resentment of MacMurray's presence on the reservation, and his unyielding, harsh treatment of the conservative Indians who opposed his orders, serve to emphasize the contrasting attitudes between the military and civil authorities at this time, at least for the Yakima Reservation. Milroy's letters (in the "Wilbur Correspondence"; see "Government Documents . . ." below) and his reports of 1884 and 1885 to the Commissioner of Indian Affairs are among the best sources to draw on for understanding the polarities of policy and attitudes among government officials toward the Indians under their jurisdiction. Mooney [163] drew heavily on MacMurray's reports in developing his study of the rise of the late nineteenth-century Indian millenarian cults as the result of dissatisfaction and deprivation. Symons [243] provided a detailed description of the Columbia River from the Canadian border to the mouth of the Snake River in his examination of the eastern Plateau authorized by General Miles before MacMurray's inspection tour.

Shortly after Nez Perce Chief Joseph's defeat in 1877, General Oliver O. Howard, in command of the Department of the Columbia, found himself involved in several other hostile incidents: the murder of the Perkinses in 1878 by renegades (mistakenly thought to be Yakimas) roaming the Rattlesnake Hills; the restiveness of Smohalla and his followers; and Chief Moses's refusal to live on the Yakima Reservation, demanding a reservation of his own for his Columbia-Sinkiuse people. General Howard's own recollections of these events [115], as part of his experiences among "our hostile Indians," was written for a popular market and is less scholarly than anecdotal. Ruby and Brown's *Half-Sun on the Columbia* [200] was also written for popular reading but contains a good section on the role of Moses as a young warrior in the Yakima wars. Ekland [70] has written an important "policy" article with insights into the legal position of the Indians, the corruption in the Indian Service, and the historic roles of Smohalla, Moses, and Wilbur during the unrest of 1878–79. Two early subsidized works that cover events of this period are Lockley [143] and Fuller [85].

In the midst of growing resentment against the autocratic regimes of the Indian agents and against interference with traditional customs and beliefs, the Yakima Indians continued to guard zealously their rights to reservation land and to secure off-reservation Indian homesteads. These rights were placed in jeopardy as public pressures for private ownership of land, including reservations, culminated with passage of the General Allotment Act of 1887, completely abrogating the original treaty provisons to maintain spatial and social exclusiveness for Indians by means of reservations. The act was legislated as a means to eliminate the Indian "problem" by encouraging private ownership of land and thereby promoting cultural assimilation. The unallotted portion of the reservation would be opened to Whites, who could then exert a "civilizing" influence on their Indian neighbors. With the breakup of tribal land tenure, tribal governments could be liquidated, reservations could be terminated, and the government could end its services. Ironically, supporters of the Allotment Act ignored the statements of perceptive military officers, reservation agents, and the Indians themselves that many of the Indian problems, such as prostitution, venereal disease, drunkenness, and poverty appeared to be directly associated with proximity to White towns or trading centers.

The practice of issuing allotments to individuals on the Yakima Reservation was not entirely new but had been incorporated into the treaty provisions as a tactical strategy to encourage farming. Relander [187] describes an 1862 map of the Yakima agency found in the National Archives that shows parcels of land already allotted to individuals. In his annual report to the Commissioner of Indian Affairs for 1871, Brunot recommended that further patents be issued to families who were cultivating land. This trend continued throughout Wilbur's term as agent.

Major issues arose among the Yakima Indians themselves over the issues of enforced allotments, sale of reservation land to Whites, and opening of the reservation. Agent Priestly reported on the open factionalism among the Yakimas over private ownership of land. Those who farmed favored allotment; those who used large tracts of tribal land for grazing horses or cattle, and the so-called wild Indians, opposed allotment. The majority of Yakima Indians were reluctant to accept allotments. Relander [187] and the Yakima Tribal Council [291] have pointed to the pressures imposed by the government on those opposed to allotments. Agent Erwin's annual report for 1895 noted that some Indians still refused allotments in spite of repressive enforcement policy. This report is also instructive in noting the various items used to distinguish "civilized" from "wild" Indians. And the split between reservation factions continued.

While the majority of Yakima Indians finally accepted allotments, many continued to oppose the sale of unallotted reservation lands, refusing to comply with the government's offer to buy their "surplus" acreage. This ongoing battle to retain reservation land as "tribal property" and the problems of land alienation through sale to non-Indians are reviewed in detail in McWhorter [153, 154], Relander [187], and Yakima Tribal Council [291]. Deutsch [64] explores White conquest of native lands from 1880 to 1912.

The turbulent postallotment period was also marked by political and legal battles over rights to water for irrigation projects and fishing rights. Agent Priestly addressed the difficulty created for Indians by irrigation projects that drew water to off-reservation land in his annual report of 1889. Agent Lynch further protested that irrigation benefited only non-Indians. Indian Office reports for the years 1874, 1882, and 1893 were also concerned with irrigation problems. McWhorter [153, 154, 155] has presented the best and most well-documented summary of what he termed "the crime against the Yakimas." Eventually the Yakimas established their primacy in water rights, but by that time much of prime irrigation farmlands had been sold, and the irrigation ditches benefited mostly non-Indians.

Allotment and the subsequent sale or lease of Indian lands accomplished what the "genocide" of epidemics, war, and bootlegged alcohol had not been able to do: a systematic "ethnocide" brought about by a loss of Indian identity with the loss of land, and a reservation split into divisive internal factions. Indian-White relations also worsened as fraudulent land deals were promoted, Indian rights were ignored or abrogated, and litigation remained unresolved. An inevitable checkerboard pattern began to take shape as non-Indians established holdings among Indian allotments. McWhorter [153] wrote that by 1913 practically all of the agriculturally productive land on the reservation was occupied by Whites, either through leases or through sale of allotments. Speculators and land developers were active, new towns were growing, stimulated by the railroad that operated right through the reservation, and land settlement continued at a rapid pace. Indians were principally picking crops, freighting, or working at other kinds of day labor.

Rights to fish at aboriginal fishing stations were also threatened as Whites homesteaded on lands adjoining the fisheries, refusing the Indians access to their accustomed fishing stations. Two famous cases, in 1886 and 1905, are the principal subjects of the annual reports of the Commissioner of Indian Affairs for those years. One of the best accounts on fishing rights is an article by Francis Garrecht [88], United States attorney, who defended Yakima Indian fishing rights in a famous case involving two Yakimas, Meninock and Wallahee. In 1915 Garrecht was adopted and made an honorary Yakima chief. He preserved for posterity Chief Meninock's speech on Yakima creation beliefs, given as part of trial testimony. Armstrong [6] has included it in her anthology of famous Indian speeches.

Two additional references address the problems of this period. Garrand and Kowrach [87] have edited the correspondence of Augustine Laure, a Jesuit priest appointed to the station of North Yakima in 1890, who describes the complexities of the Indian language, their camps, and their customs with the perception of a missionary. Trimble [252] makes an interesting comparison between American and British policies in the treatment of the Indians in the Pacific Northwest, quoting from the speech of a Yakima orator at Fort Simcoe in 1862 and raising some insightful questions about both systems.

There have been few studies on the modern reservation situation other than those conducted by various tribal committees and branches of government on their own programs and their implementation. The Yakima Nation tribal council overall economic development plan [288] summarizes much of tribal activity up to this time. Prodipto Roy [197] has provided a well-documented assessment of the socioeconomic status of the Yakima Nation, and Garretson's master's thesis [89] analyzes the reasons for rejection of the Indian Reorganization Act by the Yakima Indians.

Homer Barnett's manuscript on the Yakima Indians in 1942 [12] is a study of social adjustments, factionalism between longhair conservatives and progressives, education, economic conditions, and anti-White sentiments that he found being expressed on the reservation at that time. Much of Barnett's material is summarized and discussed by Fitch in his doctoral dissertation [78], a later examination of the economic development of the reservation economy and Indian and non-Indian relations since the influx of outsiders became a major influence on economics beginning in 1900.

The findings of the Indian Claims Commission [256, 257] contain a wealth of information on aboriginal tribal identities and locations as well as a record of the land claims of the Yakimas. It is worth noting that, in 1904, 294,000 acres that had been excluded from reservation boundaries because of an erroneous survey were returned to the tribe, and another 27,000 acres, including sacred Mount Adams, were also returned in 1972 after years of litigation [289]. Since 1954 the Yakima Nation has attempted to consolidate tribal holdings through the systematic purchasing of trust patent allotments that may be offered for sale by heirs. Recent tribal investment programs are described in *The Land of the Yakimas* [171], a tribal publication.

Two psychological studies are also available: Krause [134] has investigated drinking patterns on the Yakima Reservation, and Schuster [210] utilizes children's drawings to study differences (if any) of expressions of "Indianness" in the drawings of Indian and non-Indian schoolchildren on the reservation over a ten-year period.

General Histories

Most histories of the Yakima people are concerned with the period from 1853 to 1859, the time span of events leading up to the treaty council of 1855, the Yakima War of 1855–56, the brief period of truce, and the final Yakima War of 1858. A few histories also include the missionary period before the advent of the reservation, from 1847 until 1855. Still less frequently, a comprehensive history before White contact to the twentieth century is presented, such as is found in the work of Splawn [225], an early settler who can be credited with the first full-length account of Yakima history in a classic biography of the great Yakima chief Kamiakin. Splawn traces events as related by Indian legend and other sources from precontact times through the treaty period and Yakima wars, the opening of the reservation, and the early days of the first cattle drives and settlements in the Yakima Valley, up to the 1880s. While typifying a genre of reminiscences that tends to mix fact with fancy, Splawn's firsthand account of his coming to the Yakima country as a youth, where he settled in the cattle business by 1861 and opened a trading post in the Kittitas Valley in 1870, makes for spicy anecdotal history—autobiography as well as historical biography.

Many regional journals include historical articles on Yakima-White relations. Prominent among these are the *Oregon Historical Quarterly*, published from 1900 to the present, and the *Washington Historical Quarterly*, published from 1907 until 1935, when it became the *Pacific Northwest Quarterly*, continuing as such to the present.

Most popular knowledge of the Yakimas is through early historians such as Bancroft [10] or Victor [267]. Victor collected pioneer accounts of the wars and wrote for Bancroft as well as for the state of Oregon. Volume 31 of Bancroft's *Works*, titled *History of Washington, Idaho, and Montana*, covers 1845 to 1889 and is written from the typical ethnocentric, pioneer-biased viewpoint of early settlers. Accounts by native Americans are completely unrepresented. The Yakima material in chapters 4 and 5 contains errors both of fact and of interpretation, which unfortunately have become perpetuated in subsequent histories by Victor [267] and others.

The subsidized subscription works of the late nineteenth and early twentieth century, written to glorify the early settlers, are uneven in reliability and reflect the patronage of their supporters. W. D. Lyman has contributed two chapters to the two-volume *History of the Pacific Northwest* edited by Elwood Evans [74], which typifies this genre, as does Lyman's [146] *History of the Yakima Valley*. C. A. Snowden's multivolume *History of Washington* [221] is well written and based on more careful research than most histories of this period. Unfortunately, Snowden omits all references to original sources, even for quoted material, and his interpretations reflect the typical pro territorial government, anti regular army biases that do not accurately represent the primary sources. Fred Lockley's *History of the Columbia River Valley* [143], although a subscription work, concentrates more on human-interest stories and unrecorded sidelights of history as told to the author. Lockley's account of the fight at the Cascades is enhanced by direct reference to eyewitness accounts. George W. Fuller includes a lengthy treatment of the Yakima war years and subsequent events through the 1870s in his two published histories, *The Inland Empire* [84] and *A History of the Pacific Northwest* [85].

A few more recent general histories of the Pacific Northwest, while offering only capsule summaries of the treaty period and Yakima wars, present a more balanced treatment of the events of this significant period in Yakima history. Johansen and Gates [125] illustrate their history of the Columbia "empire" with many detailed and expertly drawn maps. Avery's [7] history of the state of Washington includes an excellent short review of events leading up to the signing of the treaty and the subsequent war, and a rare photograph of young Kamiakin. Meinig's historical geography *The Great Columbia Plain*, an important scholarly work [161], presents one of the few nonarchaeological sources that relate prehistoric cultural developments to the physical geography of eastern Washington. Meinig also discusses major historic events such as the 1855 treaty council from the point of view of a cultural geographer.

Short vignettes of the Yakima Valley's history taken from articles originally written for the Yakima *Herald-Republic,* some of them by participants in the historic events, some memoirs, and others papers written for historical societies, have been assembled by Maurice Helland [112]. These cover events from Alexander Ross's trip in 1814 to obtain horses from the Indians in Yakima Valley to the return of Mount Adams to the Yakima Reservation in 1972, more than 150 years of history in a succinct package, which makes available some attractive historical reading for secondary students. Thumbnail sketches of Yakima Valley history, written by locals, are also presented in Joseph C. Brown's *Valley of the Strong* [24]. The short articles contain informal reminiscences and personal details of life in Indian territory not to be found in formal histories.

Biographies

Few biographies have been written on the Yakimas or related peoples. The best known is the aforementioned biography by Andrew J. Splawn [225] on Kamiakin. The biography includes a basic genealogical history of Kamiakin and his family. It is also a rich source of information on other prominent Indian figures that Splawn came to know as intimates during the latter half of the nineteenth century.

William C. Brown's chronicle [25] also provides

valuable details on Kamiakin's genealogy and family history as well as information on what happened to Kamiakin's family when the chief went into exile after the wars, refusing to settle on the reservation. Brown also presented a more narrowly focused study of events related to the Indian wars and subsequent reservation history between the years 1853 and 1889. On both topics he presents "the Indian side of the story."

In a popular biography of Smohalla, the reactionary prophet of the Wanapam Indians, Relander [186] traces the life of this famous leader and that of his disciple, Puck Hyah Toot, who remained with a few other Wanapam families at Priest Rapids, refusing to leave their ancestral village site when the great Columbia River dams were being built. Their descendants continue to live today in the shadow of the Priest Rapids Dam and are a model of persistence of traditional Indian culture in the twentieth century. Most have intermarried with Yakimas and now live on the Yakima Reservation. Relander offers a somewhat romanticized version of Smohalla's life and career, but not all the accounts of Smohalla are as flattering. Major J. W. MacMurray [152], sent by General Nelson A. Miles to investigate Indian grievances in 1884, presented a fairly uncomplimentary report on Smohalla, and Splawn, [225], who knew Smohalla for twenty-five years, was equally critical of the prophet of Priest Rapids. Mooney [163] also devoted a section of his report on the Ghost Dance of 1890 to Smohalla's background and the development of the "Smohalla cult" movement and its doctrine.

A less scholarly work, but one containing useful information, is Sheller's [214] biography of Nathan Olney, who married the daughter of a Wasco chief, set up a trading post at the Dalles about 1847, was appointed agent for Indians of Oregon Territory in 1854, served with the militia during the Yakima wars, and became one of the founders of the large Olney family residing on the Yakima Reservation today. Sheller provides details on the killing of the Walla Walla chief Peu-peu-mox-mox while he was a prisoner of the Oregon Volunteers during the Yakima War of 1855, affixing the "honor" (or blame, depending on where your sympathies lie) directly upon Olney, a curious bit of historic notoriety little noted in the literature. Sheller also offered an interesting, and usually underrepresented, account of the vicissitudes of Indian-White marriage. In his enthusiasm for his Olney character, Shelley sometimes treats lesser men in a condescending tone, and his story is further marred by some inaccuracies

A biography of a different nature was written by Esther Warren [271] from material collected by her mother, who lived for fifty years among the Wishram-Wasco people at the Cascades. This is a warm and sympathetic recounting of the life of an Indian woman, Taswatha, and of the changes in the life of her family as they made adjustments to the coming of the Whites and the subsequent demise of much of their native community during the nineteenth century.

General Ethnographic Sources

For a major Plateau group, surprisingly little focused ethnographic research on the Yakimas has been published in easily available sources, and a comprehensive ethnographic summary remains to be produced. In this respect, prehistorians and historians have made more material available than have ethnographers. The paucity of references in volume 3 of Murdock and Leary [166] attests to this.

Daugherty [60] offers a capsule treatment of archaeology, ethnography, history, and modern reservation developments in his overview *The Yakima People*, written for the Indian Tribal Series. The strongest section is his summary of archaeological sequences for the Plateau, sorting out the prehistoric materials that relate to aboriginal Yakima territory, such as the important sites at Five Mile Rapids at the Dalles and near Celilo Falls, across the river from Yakima land; Lind Coulee in the eastern part of Yakima country; and the famous Marmes Rock-Shelter in southeastern Washington, once a part of Yakima territory.

Many of Curtis's photographs are sensitive portraits of Yakima life, but other scenes are too posed and artificial, hardly representative of Yakima Indians in the first decade of the twentieth century and certainly not of aboriginal culture. Although he is widely quoted as an ethnographic authority, Curtis's ethnographic materials are "shreds and patches," with an emphasis on material culture and are deficient in many significant social customs. There is little information on religious beliefs and practices, and he entirely missed the extensive longhouse ceremonial cycle, extant and popular at that time. Curtis's history of the Yakima wars [56] presents fragmentary highlights but few insights. Bancroft [9] contains a section focused on a collection of wide-ranging ethnographic data. His emphasis is also on material culture and subsistence activities, although several pages are devoted to guardian spirit powers, curing, and tribal customs.

Neither Hodge [114] nor Swanton [242]was written as an ethnographic reference; both were intended only as convenient guides to tribes of the United States and Alaska. The maps, tribal subdivisions, and linguistic information in both are dated and need revision even to be useful guides. Hodge [114] dismissed the Yakimas with a notation that "little is known," and suggested that their particular customs were substantially the same as those recorded for the Nez Perces and other Sahaptian peoples, with little regard for the differences in emphasis and development among tribal groups of the Plateau. Published in 1910, Hodge mirrors his nineteenth century predecessors such as Schoolcraft [208].

One of the earlier works that still merits attention is Albert B. Lewis's general description of the tribes of the Columbia Valley and the coast of Washington and Oregon [139]. Lewis wrote a carefully researched and well-documented survey of what was known at that time, and his ethnographic descriptions cover all aspects of tribal life on the Plateau, from linguistics and social organization to food and material culture, archaeology, mythology, rituals, burial customs, art, trade, and tribal movements.

Some of the myths, legends, and ethnographic data collected by Dr. George P. Kuykendall while he was Yakima agency physician at Fort Simcoe from 1872 to 1882, have been included in Elwood Evans's *History of the Pacific Northwest* as chapter 60, "The Indians of the Pacific Northwest" [136]. Fred Lockley's *History of the Columbia River Valley* [143] also includes some myths and traditions of the Yakimas as related by Dr. Kuykendall. A less scholarly book, but one with interesting information, is H. Dean Guie's *Tribal Days of the Yakimas* [101]. The book is short, written in simple language and printed in bold type, an appealing format as an introductory ethnography for secondary students.

Although titled *Gambling among the Yakima*, Desmond's doctoral dissertation [63] covers far more than gambling and is an important contribution, presenting one of the best reconstructions of Yakima life in the postwar years of the mid-nineteenth century. Schuster's doctoral dissertation [209] summarizes most of the published material available to date, augmented by her own extensive interviews and participation in traditional Yakima longhouse activities during fieldwork in the 1960s and early 1970s. Schuster is particularly concerned with documenting continuity between present and past traditional Yakima customs, a prime example of an ongoing, resilient, living Indian tradition with direct roots in the past. There is special focus on the structure and viability of the traditional longhouse community with its distinctive set of values. Schuster's dissertation is being prepared for publication.

Traditional Social Organization and Customs

In aboriginal times, the people known today as "Yakimas" comprised small, politically autonomous groups, joined together by informal bonds of territorial contiguity and common interests, customs, and language. The ambiguous nature of political alignments and the tendency to favor local autonomy are apparent in early accounts of Yakima political organization. By mid-nineteenth century, a division of Yakima territory, roughly along Wenas Creek, into Upper and Lower Yakima bands is reported by Gibbs [92] and corroborated by Indian Agent Robie [193]. In addition, a number of closely allied villages might be known collectively as "local bands," though there is no evidence of any permanent organizational structure.

There is some basis for the existence of limited tribal unification in historical legend dated to the 1700s and related by Splawn [225]. Splawn tells of this "confederation" of Upper Yakima–Kittitas and Middle Yakima bands down to the mouth of Toppenish Creek, accomplished by a Kittitas chief named We-ow-wicht, who is referred to by Splawn as the "fountainhead of Yakima royalty." Records confirm the existence of the chief's sons, who each exercised control in varying degrees over a particular section of this territory, and of a sister who was the mother of Kamiakin.

The village was the basic political as well as social unit, with control vested informally in a headman and his council. The earliest village descriptions for this part of the Plateau are found in the work of David Thompson [248], who described a Wenatchi fishing village as he descended the Columbia River in 1811, and in the writings of Ross [195], the fur trader with the Stuart party in 1811, who made detailed observations on the mat lodges, erected as multifamily dwellings or "longhouses" in scattered groupings along the Columbia River. Curtis [55, 56] appears to have derived much of his information on Yakima villages from Ross's journal. Townsend [250], and Gibbs [92] should be consulted for nineteenth century descriptions of permanent "winter villages" or band settlements. Desmond [63] may be consulted for descriptions of lodges, a "dance house" (communal longhouse?), and sweat lodges from 1860 to 1880.

Ray [184] is recommended for details on aboriginal village locations along the Yakima River and its tributaries. Ray's information has been extensively and meticulously recorded for location of relatively permanent villages and large, temporary camps. Somewhat different subdivisions along the lower Yakima River are recorded by Curtis [55, 56], Spier [223], and Swanton [242], basing their classification largely on the names of "local bands" along an entire tributary or stream rather than on identification of villages. These latter reports are too simplified and condensed to be of more than generalized use. Mooney incorrectly classifies some of the Upper Yakima bands as Wenatchi, an error that probably reflects the extensive intermarriage between Wenatchi and Yakima families.

Some of the earliest reports on Yakima culture told of the extensive gatherings or encampments held annually at various central areas in Yakima territory for communal activities such as root digging, trading, or fishing. The earliest account of an extensive intergroup gathering comes to us in a firsthand detailed description of an intertribal encampment in the Kittitas Valley east of present Ellensburg in early June 1814, recorded by Alexander Ross [196], clerk of the North West Company. Ross's journal entries contain a wealth of descriptive data and impressions derived from his tour of the camp, accompanied by one of the Yakima chiefs, Eyacktana, as Ross sought to recover his own horses as well as those he had come to barter for.

Writing in 1871, Splawn [225] described another annual encampment at the same great council and root grounds near Ellensburg. Splawn's observations complement Ross's earlier accounts as he describes the sporting events that follow the annual activities of digging for roots, gambling, and horse racing. Desmond [63] also gives considerable attention to descriptions of the "big time" during summer. Desmond is considerably more detailed than either of the accounts by Ross or Splawn, describing how intervillage horse racing had become a highlight at seasonal gatherings by the 1860s and presenting additional information on a large community-sponsored feast held at the encampment. Encampments were also occasions for visiting, holding councils, trading, and arranging marriages. Similar major intertribal gatherings could be found in Klikitat territory, at great trading centers such as the Dalles, and during the height of the fishing season at popular sites such as Celilo Falls.

Information on the extensive cultural relationships maintained on the Columbia Plateau between tribal peoples was first summarized by Verne F. Ray [183]. Anastasio's doctoral dissertation of 1955 identified and analyzed Plateau networks of relationships, alliances, and social organization [3]. Brunton [28] concentrated on ceremonial patterns as an integrative force for maintaining relationships. Griswold's master's thesis on aboriginal patterns of trade between the Columbia Basin and the northern Plains [99, 100] traced the spread of various items such as highly prized war bonnets borrowed from the Sioux and dance bustles from the Bannocks. Trading activities were also noted between the Plateau and Northwest Coast tribes by Gibbs [92], where horses and hides were exchanged for dried clams and precious dentalia shell.

Gatherings, encampments, trading relationships, and other social interactions were largely regulated by the food quest. Subsistence on this part of the Columbia Plateau was derived primarily by gathering wild plant food (roots and berries), by fishing (principally for salmon), and by hunting wild game. Volume 3 of the Thwaites edition of the Lewis and Clark journals [140] contains one of the best descriptions of the preparation of "salmon pemmican," describing in detail the process of drying, preserving, and storing the fish. Other early nineteenth-century reports on fishing activities can be found in Ross [195], Simpson [162, 216], and Thompson [248]. Ross also records seeing the Indians hunting for game on horseback during 1811. Mid-nineteenth-century descriptions of subsistence activities are numerous, particularly of the famous fishing stations at the Wenatchapam fishery in June and at Celilo Falls in fall. Schuster [209] summarizes much of this information found in reports such as Wilkes [276], Kane [127], Gibbs [92], and Hale [106]. Gibbs further notes that, though game had once been plentiful on the eastern slopes of the Cascades, by 1854 it was almost exhausted. Additional information on subsistence has been collected in Ray [182, 183], Curtis [56], Desmond [63], Anastasio [3], and Filloon [77].

Resources on general customs and traditions of the Yakimas are few. Filloon [77] has written a brief but good article on some early twentieth-century subsistence skills, such as picking and drying berries and roasting camas bulbs, preparing cedar bark and other baskets, and tanning hides. Filloon also describes a berry feast in a longhouse, sweat houses and bathing, racing and gambling, and other traditional customs. Strong [236] wrote principally about the Indians of the Pacific Coast, among whom he began to live in 1850.

He presents a sympathetic narrative "through Indian eyes" of Yakima country, where he hunted in 1854. Curtis [56] details several Yakima customs relating to ear piercing, naming, marriage, and canoe burials. McWhorter [153] contains a rare photograph taken in 1911 of a wedding trade. Thompson [248] and Splawn [225] both describe burial customs, and Strong [235] adds to knowledge on the production of mats and baskets. Leechman [137] and Harrington [111] have collected information on the unique "calendar strings" of the Yakima women, the biographical records of an individual's history preserved by means of knots, beads, yarn, and other materials to mark the special happenings in a woman's lifetime.

More complete information on life-cycle events, social and ritual occasions, and general cultural traditions of the Yakima Indians will be available when Schuster's manuscript is revised and published.

One of the principal aesthetic contributions of Plateau peoples has been their basketry. As a general source, Mason [159] is still the classic work on American Indian basketry. The major study of basketry from the middle Columbia River is to be found in Haeberlin, Teit, and Roberts [104]. Recent popular interest in basketry has led to the publication of a new journal, *American Indian Basketry*. The first issue features two excellent articles, one by John M. Gogol [96] on Columbia River basketry and the other by Mary Schlick [206], based on her extensive research on a Wasco bag collected by Lewis and Clark in 1805. Outstanding articles were also written for the second issue by Gogol [97] and by Schlick [207] on flat twinged "cornhusk" bags and hats. Old baskets are photographed in their natural surroundings in Lobb's extravagant photo essay *Indian Baskets of the Northwest Coast* [142].

Yakima Indian Religion

Yakima religious beliefs and practices constitute an integral part of the traditional social system to this day. For discussion, two distinct spheres of religious activity can be distinguished: the guardian spirit complex and curing, on the one hand, and *Wa'shat*, the longhouse or "seven drum" or "Indian religion," which does not utilize "doctoring," on the other.

The guardian spirit complex of activities probably represents the older religious system. It includes the vision quest and other means of acquiring power, "medicine sings" or "winter sings" when spirit powers are expressed in song and dance, the sweat lodge, sweat bathing, and shamanism, and the rituals of medicine doctors for diagnosing and curing supernaturally derived illnesses and spirit sickness. There are also concepts that the spiritual world contains pranksters, potentially dangerous beings, as well as guardian spirit helpers, and a belief in an impersonal spirit or life force, "like a warm breath rising."

There is little in the published literature on this aspect of Yakima religion. Bancroft [9] has written briefly on guardian spirit powers, Splawn [225] contains a rare description of a ritual performed by a medicine doctor to bring on the warm Chinook winds, and Desmond [63] briefly discusses the role of the *twati* or medicine doctor. Gibbs [92], Curtis [56], and Blanchet [21] note a few beliefs, and Helland [112] has published a brief account by Kuykendall on medicine doctors. Alvord [2] points to the precarious position of the medicine doctor, who may be killed if unsuccessful in his treatment of the patient, a fact corroborated in Yakima Agency reports for the 1880s. Schuster [209] has compiled some incidents related by Yakima informants of their own experiences with guardian spirit powers, spirit illness, curing, and the past and present role of the medicine doctor in Yakima society, but a comprehensive study remains to be done.

The second domain of religious activities is known today as *Wa'shat*, the longhouse or "Indian religion," which includes a large complex of ceremonial activities related both to "rites of passage" (such as namings, wedding trades, modern marriage rites, first products feasts, funerals, memorial ceremonies, first dancing rites, and other significant events in the life of an individual) and to calendric rituals (such as first foods feasts, commemorative rites, and the regular "Sunday dance").

One of the best primary accounts of longhouse ceremonialism was written by Major J. W. MacMurray [151, 152] in 1884. MacMurray had the opportunity to witness a number of longhouse ceremonials at Celilo and Umatilla in Oregon, at Tumwater, at Smohalla's longhouse at Priest Rapids, and at various places on the Yakima Reservation. His observations on prophets and followers of the Dreamer religion are some of the most complete records available [152]. Much of Mooney's information on Yakima longhouse rituals in his publication on the Ghost Dance of 1890 [163] was derived from MacMurray's reports. A description of a "salmon feast" held in April was also related to Mooney by Charles Ike, a Christianized Yakima, whose translations for Mooney were apparently reinterpreted to fit a Christian mode and should be used with caution.

One of the earliest descriptions of longhouse ritual was made by Dr. Gairdner [86] while at Fort Walla Walla in 1835. The works by Parker [177], Townsend [250], and Bonneville (in Irving [118]) contain brief descriptions of communal longhouse ceremonies among the Nez Perces and the Walla Wallas. Wood [280] also noted a longhouse ceremony he attended in 1879. Filloon [77] has written a good article on a berry feast (among other ethnographic notes) in the early twentieth century, and Julia Seelatsee [212], a Yakima Indian, presents a short account of a first foods feast among the Yakimas about the Christmas season. The rituals described by Guie [101] are presented in a way particularly suitable for the younger reader.

A solid case for deriving the *Wa'shat* religion from a revivalist religious development known as Prophet cults or the Prophet Dance has been developed by Spier [222] in his extensively researched essay on the cult movement and its derivatives. Many variations of the movement emerged during the nineteenth century, the main period of Prophet Dance activities. Some of the better known of these movements, besides the *Wa'shat* religion, include the two Ghost Dance movements of 1870 and 1890, the "dreamers" of the middle Columbia plateau (including the Smohalla cult of Priest Rapids), the Indian Shakers of the Northwest, and the Feather cult of the middle Columbia plateau. Prophets became known as "dreamers" because of the trancelike state in which they received their visions. Most prophecies followed a basic formula of destruction, resurrection, and a golden era of salvation for loyal followers, a familiar millenarian pattern with both Christian and indigenous components. Many of the features of modern *Wa'shat* ritual have been noted in early Prophet Dance ceremonialism by Schuster [209]. DuBois [68] also presented field data in support of the derivations of *Wa'shat* from Spier's earlier "Christianized" Prophet Dance. Today *Wa'shat* is perceived as the tribal or indigenous Indian religion on the Yakima Reservation, and Christian elements (such as bell ringing) have become a thoroughly integrated part of an Indian religion.

During the latter half of the nineteenth century, prophecies of dreamers became more anti-White, and nativistic cults began to emerge, born of disillusion with broken treaties, military campaigns, suppression of Indian religion and language, and deprivations that followed removal of Indians to reservations. The

Dreamer religion of the middle Columbia Plateau was one manifestation of these movements, though its peaceful nature is now apparent. Among the variants was the Smohalla cult, the focus of Relander's *Drummers and Dreamers* [186] and given prominence in Mooney's major work on the Ghost Dance [163].

Smohalla was actually only one of a series of prophets and dreamers who gathered adherents at this time. Relander [186] errs in describing Smohalla as the founder and head of the *Wà shat* leaders in longhouses throughout the Plateau, including the famous longhouse leader at Union Gap, the Yakima chief Kotiahkan, and Smohalla's service ws only one of many variants in this religious development. Besides previously cited writers, Smohalla's cult has been extensively documented by Huggins, [116], Crowder [52], Fuller [85], Howard [115], and others.

The definitive work on the Indian Shaker religion has been written by Homer Barnett [11]. Founded in 1882 on Puget Sound, this messianic cult was first established east of the Cascades in 1899. There are now three churches representing several sects on the Yakima Reservation, all of which enjoy considerable followings. The Shaker religion represents a syncretism of fundamental Christianity, Catholicism, and native Indian elements derived from shamanistic "curing" practices and the old Prophet Dance. The "shake" or power to cure is regarded by many traditional Indians as analogous to the power of an Indian doctor or shaman. Fitzpatrick [79] has summarized the development and role of the Shaker church on the Yakima Reservation in her master's thesis. Ruby [199] presents an article on a Shaker healing service, and Harmon [110] adds material on the Shaker church at the Dalles, visited by Yakima Shakers.

The Feather religion, or Feather cult, is also an Indian "curing" religion. Founded about 1904 by Jake Hunt, a Klikitat, the cult spread to the Yakima Reservation about 1905. Like the Indian Shakers, members of the Feather cult seek to perform cures in homes, and the rituals are focused primarily on combating alcoholism. The best comprehensive study of the origin and development of the Feather cult was researched and written by Cora DuBois [68].

Mythology

The earliest corpus of Indian myths to be collected in the Yakima region was assembled by George Gibbs in the course of his exploratory work for the Northern Pacific Railroad Survey during the 1850s [39]. While he was Yakima agency physician at Fort Simcoe from 1872 to 1882, Dr. G. P. Kuykendall was asked by Major J. W. Powell of the Bureau of American Ethnology to collect folklore, legends, and mythology [136]. J. M. Cornelison [46], missionary to Umatilla, published his *Weyekin Stories* in 1911. Franz Boas [22, 76] edited a memoir of Salishan and Sahaptin folktales for the American Folk-Lore Society in 1917. All these early collections, although valuable introductions to the field of mythology, are only modest samplings of the rich oral traditions of the Yakimas.

The first extensive corpus of myths, systematically obtained in the Klikitat, Upper Cowlitz, and Kittitas dialects, was published in the original Indian languages with interlinear translations, followed by English versions, by Melville Jacobs [119] in 1929. These were followed by a more comprehensive two-volume series of Northwest Sahaptin texts: part 1 [122] consisting of the English translations and part 2 [124] a transcription of the original Sahaptin texts as dictated to Jacobs by informants at various times between 1926 and 1930. Until the recent Yakima tribal projects on oral traditions, these were the most reliable data on mythology and folklore for the Yakimas to date.

During the last decade, the Yakima Indian Nation has initiated several oral history projects that have resulted in an invaluable collection of myths, folktales, and legends on tape from tribal elders, the traditional storytellers and repositories of tribal history and wisdom. Many of these legends, recounted in Yakima dialects, have been translated into English. The first of these projects, sponsored by the Consortium of Johnson O'Malley Committees of Region IV under the direction of Virginia Beavert [14] has culminated in the publication of a noteworthy book of legends, *The Way It Was: Anaku Iwacha, Yakima Indian Legends*. These important firsthand accounts are enhanced by illustrations drawn by young tribal members.

Several modern, shortened versions of classic folktales can be found in the collections of Bunnell [29] and Ella Clark [37, 38]. These include the most popular legends of the Cascade Mountain peaks and of the Cascades of the Columbia River.

Linguistics and Language Learning

The Yakimas speak a Northern Sahaptin language, part of the Penutian language phylum, closely related to variants of Sahaptin spoken by the Klickitat, Wanapam, Walla Walla, Palouse, Umatilla, Upper Cowlitz (*táidnapam*), *skín*, Tenino-Wyam, and Warm Springs Indians. Northern Sahaptin is more distantly related to other Sahaptain languages spoken by the Nez Perces, Cayuses, Klamath-Modocs, and Molalas, and to Chinookan-speakers such as the Wishram and Wasco.

The earliest systematic linguistic work was done by Horatio Hale [106], philologist with the Wilkes expedition of 1838–42, whose report contained linguistic material on the "Yakimas," among other Sahaptian speakers. Two rare early grammars and dictionaries were compiled by Catholic missionaries, the first to establish a mission among the Yakima Indians. Father Pandosy's grammar and dictionary of the Sahaptin language [176] is based mainly on Kittitas or the *pshwánwapam* dialect. Father St. Onge [204] produced the first printed alphabet of the Yakima language, also in French, along with prayers and catechism, published in 1872. St. Onge distinguished four dialects of Yakima that he called Sapsikuatpama, Timash, Mamachatumki, and Yakamiei Mianashmamiel. His primer and catechism is in the *mámashat* dialect, the same dialect that is being used today to teach the Yakima language in the public school system on the reservation. Copies of both these rare works can be found in the Pacific Northwest Collections of the University of Washington Library in Seattle.

Melville Jacobs's grammar and lexicon [120] of Northern Sahaptin was obtained from speakers of Klickitat and *táidnapam* (Upper Cowlitz) dialects, closely related to those of the Yakima proper. This work remains a definitive study for this language group. Jacobs followed his grammar with an important compilation of kinship terms [121] and an extensive collection of folklore and mythology (discussed above). To cap his eminence in the field, Jacobs [123] published a landmark article on historic relationships of Indian languages in Oregon and Washington, including Sahaptin.

In an interesting study combining physical anthropology with linguistics, Frederick Hulse [117] compared Yakima blood group types with those of two Salish-speaking groups in order to investigate language differences as a barrier to gene flow. Hulse concluded that distinctions between Yakima data and those of the Salish tribes point to less contact between these peoples than between Yakimas and tribal groups to the east, which share more gene frequencies. Hulse also suggested the hypothesis of greater contact between the Yakimas and northwestern Plains peoples than with the Coast and northern Plateau Salish-speaking tribes.

Some recent comparisons between Nez Perce and Northern Sahaptin have been completed by Āoki [4], whose studies have also extended to comparisons of Nez Perce and Proto-Sahaptin kinship terms [5]. Other recent contributions to linguistics that deserve attention include Rigsby's doctoral dissertation on linguistic relations in the southern Plateau [192], his study of Sahaptin vowel systems [191], and Thelma E. Weeks's analysis of paralinguistic and registral aspects of Yakima children's speech [273]. Rigsby's work is particularly important, since he has instructed in Sahaptin language workshops on the Yakima Reservation and helped to train native language specialists.

The Yakima Indian Nation Education Division and the Johnson O'Malley Consortium on the reservation have been responsible for preparing curricula and other teaching materials for learning the Yakima language. Some of the latest include *Multi-Cultural Early Childhood Curriculum* [290] and a *Mamashat Sinwit* [*Language*] *Teachers' Guide* [43].

The Sahaptin River Tribes Consortium, composed of representatives from the Yakima, Nez Perce, Warm Springs, Colville, and Umatilla groups, has developed a printed alphabet for tribes sharing the Sahaptin language [203], which will permit further cooperation and coordination of efforts to preserve and promote language-learning for future generations.

Related Plateau Tribal Groups

The artist Paul Kane made two trips west between 1845 and 1848, recording his impressions in sketches and in a daily journal. Although he makes no mention of the Yakimas, Kane has left a notable ethnographic record on houses, fishing, and other customs of tribes he met along that stretch of the Columbia River from Colville and the Okanogan country past Fort Walla Walla, the Cascades and the Dalles to Fort Vancouver. These tribal groups included the Nez Perces, Walla Wallas, Cayuses, Chinooks, Klikitats, Skinpahs (*skin*), "Shutes," and others. Kane spent the most time among the Walla Wallas, and his description of a winter house is invaluable [127, 266].

Details of tribal distribution and major linguistic boundaries (Salish-Sahaptian-Chinook) for the middle Columbia area of the Plateau during the late eighteenth and early nineteenth centuries are provided in Jacobs [120, 123], Ray [182, 184], Spier [223], and Meinig [161]. There is considerable agreement on general territorial divisions. The distribution map and accompanying text of Spier [223] are reproduced in volume 2 of the Indian Claims Commission report [257]. Verne Ray, an expert witness for these hearings, also produced a map of tribal territories [182, fig. 5] that, while similar, appears to be more accurate and has gained wider acceptance than Spier's.

Typical early ethnographies have tended to emphasize material culture. Early fieldwork was conducted by James Teit [245] for a brief period in 1908 on the Moses Columbia-Sinkiuses and the Wenatchi-Pisquous, that Teit classified as "Middle Columbia Salish." This ethnography is significant for an early description of trading activities at the great trading center of the Dalles and for cultural information on the Salish-speaking Wenatchis to the north of the Yakimas, with many close ties through marriage. Teit [246] describes some parallel customs for the Salishan tribes of the western Plateau, including the Okanagon, Sanpoil, Colville, Lake, Coeur d'Alene, Flathead, Spokane, Kalispel, and Pend d'Oreilles groups. Ray [181] also treats the Sanpoils and Nespelems. The Sinkaietks or Southern Okanagons are the focus of Cline, et al. [41].

Ruby and Brown have produced two first-rate studies of Plateau groups. Their *Half-Sun on the Columbia* [200] is an excellent biography of Chief Moses, leader of the Columbia-Sinkiuses in the latter half of the nineteenth century. Although written as a biography of Moses, it includes critical events on the Yakima Reservation and in the Yakima Valley affecting the course of reservation history during the 1870s until Moses agreed to locate his people on his own reservation in north-central Washington. Their 1972 work [201] is an account of the Cayuse Indians, particularly important for the impact of the Whitman massacre in the 1840s on later Plateau history.

Spier and Sapir's [224] ethnographic survey of the Chinookan-speaking Wishram and Wasco people, many of whom now live on the Yakima Reservation, was principally conducted during the first quarter of this century between 1905 and 1925. In a later study of the Wishram-Wascos, David French [81] synthesizes the known ethnographic information and presents a detailed analysis of culture change since White contact, in a chapter in Spicer's edited volume *Perspectives in American Indian Culture Change.*

Contemporary social ceremonialism has been analyzed by Katherine French [82] for the Tenino on the Warm Springs Reservation in Oregon, a Sahaptian people closely related to the Yakima by marriage ties, by language, and by customs.

The culturally conservative Wanapams of Priest Rapids on the Columbia River south of Vantage are also closely related to the Yakimas through marriage. These people are the focus of Relander's *Drummers and Dreamers* [186].

The Nez Perces on the southeastern borders of the Plateau have probably been the object of more extensive interest and investigation than any other Plateau society, principally due to the fame of Chief Joseph and his people's unsuccessful fight against dispossession of their lands, and their unsuccessful flight to freedom. Two classic ethnohistories of the Nez Perces have been written, one by Haines [105]; the other by Josephy [126]. Josephy has assembled an effective, moving, historical narrative of Joseph and the Nez Perces, synthesizing much of the useful documentary materials. His ethnographic data are somewhat marred by the number of inaccuracies, but his story of Joseph's loss of his beloved Wallola Valley in Northeastern Oregon and his gallant leadership of his band in an attempt to evade military forces and gain their freedom in Canada remains one of the best general summaries of early contact and confrontation in Nez Perce history.

Walker [268] fills in neglected ethnographic information on social organization and on religion, especially shamanism and the guardian spirit quest, and analyzes the effect of White contact on Nez Perce religion and politics. The most recent comprehensive work is a culture history written by the Nez Perces themselves, one of the first Indian-written tribal histories from the Indian point of view (see Slickpoo and Walker [217]). The book is particularly valuable for nineteenth- and early twentieth-century photographs, many from private Nez Perce collections.

Earl Swanson, et al. have provided a useful discussion of "Cultural Relations between the Plateau and the Great Basin" [241].

Yakima Tribal Publications

The Yakima Indian Nation, largely under the auspices of the Tribal Council, has been responsible for producing and publishing several compact overviews and summaries of tribal customs, history, modern economic development, and educational programs on the reservation today. The first of these was produced on the occasion of the treaty centennial, *The Yakimas: Treaty*

Centennial, 1855–1955 [291]. This was followed in 1962 by a "historiette" entitled *Strangers on the Land* [187], written by Relander and others about the confrontations of the Yakima Nation involving retention of its land, fisheries, customs, and sovereignty while resisting pressures to assimilate into the larger society. The text provides some ethnographic details and contains a wealth of information on reservation history, touching on primary references that should provide many suggestions as avenues for further research. *A Primer of the Yakimas* appeared the same year [287].

Yakima Indian Nation [255], published in 1971, is largely a capsule treatment of the present-day reservation with some cultural background and history. A popular booklet commemorating the occasion of the restoration of Mount Adams to the Reservation, correcting an early survey error, was produced in 1972 [289]. Most recent is *The Land of the Yakimas* [171], compiled by Robert E. Pace of the Yakima Nation media center and edited by the Kamiakin Research Institute Cultural Heritage Center in 1977. This covers brief highlights of Yakima history from the time of Lewis and Clark but is largely a sketch of the contemporary Yakima Indian Nation, its Tribal Council and other governing bodies, tribal services, educational and social programs, and economic development enterprises.

A tribally sponsored newspaper, the *Yakima Nation Review*, was founded in May 1970 and is published bimonthly at Toppenish, Washington, the agency town.

ALPHABETICAL LIST AND INDEX

*Denotes items suitable for secondary school students

Item No.		Essay Page No.
[1]	Aikens, C. Melvin. 1978. "Plateau." In *Ancient Native Americans*, ed. Jesse D. Jennings, pp. 164–81. San Francisco: W. H. Freeman.	(11, 12)
[2]	Alvord, B. 1884. "The Doctor-Killing in Oregon." *Harper's New Monthly Magazine* (February, pp. 364–66.	(89)
[3]	Anastasio, Angelo. 1972. "The Southern Plateau: An Ecological Analysis of Intergroup Relations." *Northwest Anthropological Research Notes* 6:109–229.	(20, 22, 85, 86)
[4]	Aoki, Haruo. 1962. "Nez Perce and Northern Sahaptin: A Binary Comparison." *International Journal of American Linquistics* 28(3):172–82.	(97)
[5]	———. 1966. "Nez Perce and Proto-Sahaptian Kinship Terms." *International Journal of American Linquistics* 32(4):357–68.	(97)

*[6]   Armstrong, Virginia Irving, comp.
1971. *I Have Spoken: American History
through the Voices of the Indians.* Chicago:
Swallow Press.   (71)

[7]   Avery, Mary. 1961. *History and Government of the State of Washington.* Seattle:
University of Washington Press.   (38, 75)

*[8]   Ballou, Robert. 1938. *Early Klickitat Val-
ley Days.* Goldendale, Wash.: Gold-
endale Sentinel.   (53)

[9]   Bancroft, Hubert Howe. 1888. *History
of Oregon.* Vol. 2. *1848–1888.* Vol. 30 of
The Works of H. H. Bancroft. San Francisco: History Company.   (80, 88)

[10]   ———. 1890. *History of Washington,
Idaho, and Montana, 1845–1889.* Vol. 31
of *The Works of H. H. Bancroft.* San
Francisco: History Company.   (38, 55, 74)

[11]   Barnett, Homer G. 1957. *Indian Shakers, a Messianic Cult of the Pacific Northwest.* Carbondale: University of Southern Illinois Press.   (92)

[12]   ———. 1969. *The Yakima Indians in
1942.* Eugene: Department of Anthropology, University of Oregon.   (72)

[13] Beall, Thomas B. 1917. "Pioneer Reminiscences." *Washington Historical Quarterly* 8(2):83– 90. (55)

*[14] Beavert, Virginia. 1974. *The Way It Was: Anaku Iwacha, Yakima Indian Legends.* Consortium of Johnson O'Malley Committees of Region IV, State of Washington. Franklin Press. (94)

[15] Bischoff, William N., S.J. 1945. *The Jesuits in Old Oregon, 1840–1940.* Caldwell, Idaho: Caxton Printers. (29)

[16] ———. 1949. "The Yakima Campaign of 1856." *Mid-America* 31:163–208. (47, 50)

[17] ———. 1950. "The Yakima Indian War, 1855–1856: A Problem in Research." *Pacific Northwest Quarterly* 41:162–69. (51)

[18] ———. 1950. "The Yakima Indian War: 1855–1856," Ph.D. diss., Loyola University. (49)

[19] ———. 1950. "Tracing Manuscript Sources." *Oregon Historical Quarterly* 51:156–63. (50)

[20]　Bischoff, William N., S.J., and Charles M. Gates. 1943. "The Jesuits and Their Coeur d'Alene Treaty of 1858." *Pacific Northwest Quarterly* 34:169–81.　(57)

[21]　Blanchet, Francis N. 1878. *Historical Sketches of the Catholic Church in Oregon during the Past Forty Years.* Portland, Oreg.: Catholic Centennial Press.　(89)

[22]　Boas, Franz, ed. 1917. *Folk-Tales of Salishan and Sahaptin Tribes.* Collected by James A. Teit, Marian K. Gould, Livingston Farrand, and Herbert J. Spinden. Memoirs of the American Folk-Lore Society 11. Lancaster, Pa.: American Folk-Lore Society. See [76].　(93)

[23]　Browman, David L., and David A. Munsell. 1969. "Columbia Plateau Pre-History: Cultural Development and Impinging Influences." *American Antiquity* 34:249–64.　(15)

*[24]　Brown, Joseph C., ed. 1974. *Valley of the Strong: Stories of Yakima and Central Washington History.* Yakima, Wash.: Wescoast.　(76)

*[25]　Brown, William Compton. 1961. *The

Indian Side of the Story. Spokane: C. W. Hill. (38, 51, 53ff.)

[26] Browne, J. Ross. 1858. "Indian War in Oregon and Washington Territories. Special Report to the Secy. of War and the Secy. of the Interior, Dated December 4, 1857." 35th Cong., 1st Sess., House Exec. Doc. no. 38, pp. 1–66 (serial set 955). Also in Sen. Exec. Doc. no 40, serial set 929. (52)

[27] Brunot, Felix R. 1871. "Minutes of a Council Held With Simco Indians at Their Reservation." In *Report of the Commissioner of Indian Affairs for the Year 1871*, pp. 131–35. Washington, D.C.: Government Printing Office. (63)

[28] Brunton, Bill B. 1968. "Ceremonial Integration in the Plateau of Northwestern North America." *Northwest Anthropological Research Notes* 2:1–28. (85)

*[29] Bunnell, Clarence O. 1933. *Legends of the Klickitats.* Portland: Metropolitan Press. (95)

[30] Burns, Robert I., S.J. 1947. "Père Joset's Account of the Indian War of

1858." *Pacific Northwest Quarterly*
38:285–314.   (57, 61)

[31]   ———. 1966. *The Jesuits and the Indian
Wars of the Northwest.* New Haven: Yale
University Press.   (51, 60)

[32]   Butler, Robert B. 1957. "Art of the
Lower Columbia Valley." *Archaeology*
10(3):156–65.   (16)

[33]   ———. 1965. "Perspectives on the
Prehistory of the Lower Columbia Val-
ley." *Tebiwa: Journal of the Idaho State
Museum,* vol. 8, no. 1.   (15)

[34]   ———. 1965. "The Structure and
Function of the Old Cordilleran Culture Concept." *American Anthropologist*,
n.s., 67:1120–31.   (15)

[35]   Cain, Harvey Thomas. 1950. *Petroglyphs
of Central Washington.* Seattle: University
of Washington Press.   (16)

[36]   Chadwick, S. J. 1908. "Colonel Steptoe's Battle." *Washington Historical Quarterly* 2(4)333–43.   (55)

[37]   Clark, Ella. 1952. "The Bridge of the

Gods in Fact and Fancy." *Oregon Historical Quarterly* 53:29–38.   (95)

[38] ———. 1953. *Indian Legends of the Pacific Northwest.* Berkeley: University of California Press.   (95)

[39] ———. 1955–56. "George Gibbs' Account of Indian Mythology in Oregon and Washington Territories." *Oregon Historical Quarterly* 56:293–325 (part 1); 57:125–67 (part 2.)   (93)

[40] Clark, Robert C. 1935. "Military History of Oregon, 1849–1859." *Oregon Historical Quarterly* 36:14–59.   (60)

[41] Cline, Walter, et al. 1938. *The Sinkaietk or Southern Okanagon of Washington.* General Series in Anthropology 6. Menasha, Wisc.: George Banta.   (99)

[42] Coan, C. F. 1922. "The Adoption of the Reservation Policy in the Pacific Northwest, 1853–1855." *Oregon Historical Quarterly* 23:1–38.   (34)

[43] Consortium of Johnson O'Malley Committees, Region IV. 1978. *Màmashat Sinwit [Language], Teachers'*

Guide. Toppenish, Wash.: Johnson
O'Malley.   (97)

[44] Cook, Sherburne F. 1955. "The
Epidemic of 1830–1833 in California
and Oregon." *University of California
Publications in American Archaeology and
Ethnology* 43:303–26.   (22)

[45] Coon, Delia M. 1923. "Klickitat Coun-
ty: Indians of and Settlement by
Whites." *Washington Historical Quarterly*
14(4):248–61.   (47)

[46] Cornelison, J. M. 1911. *Weyekin Stories:
Titwatit Weyekishnim.* San Francisco: E.
L. Mackey.   (93)

[47] Coues, Elliott, ed. 1897. *New Light on the
Early History of the Greater Northwest: The
Manuscript Journals of Alexander Henry
and of David Thompson, 1799–1814.* 3
vols. New York: Francis P. Harper.   (24)

[48] Cox, Ross. 1831. *Adventures on the Columbia River.* 2 vols. London: H. Col-
burn and R. Bentley. Reprinted, Portland: Binford and Mort, 1975.   (2, 24)

[49] Cram, Thomas J. 1859. "Topographical

Memoir of the Department of the Pacific." 35th Cong. 2d Sess. House Exec. Doc. no. 114, pp. 1–126, serial set 1014. Washington, D.C.: James B. Steedman, Printer. Reprinted, Fairfield, Wash.: Ye Galleon Press, 1978.   (46, 52, 54)

[50] Cressman, Luther S., et al. 1960. "Cultural Sequences at the Dalles, Oregon: A Contribution to Pacific Northwest History." *American Philosophical Society Transactions* 50:10.   (12)

[51] Crook, George. 1946. *General George Crook: His Autobiography*. Ed. Martin F. Schmitt. Norman: University of Oklahoma Press. Reprinted, 1963.   (55)

[52] Crowder, Stella I. 1913. "The Dreamers." *Overland Monthly* 62:607–9.   (92)

[53] Culverwell, Albert. 1955. "Stronghold in the Yakima Country: Fort Simcoe and the Indian War, 1856–1859." *Pacific Northwest Quarterly* 46:46–51.   (48)

[54] Curry, George C. 1855. "Expeditions against the Indians." In *Correspondence and Official Proceedings, Governor of Ore-*

gon Territory, George C. Curry, to the Citizens. Salem, Oreg.: Asahel Bush, Territorial Printer.   (44)

[55] Curtis, Edward Sheriff. 1911. *The Nez Perces. The Wallawalla, Umatilla, Cayuse. The Chinookan Tribes.* Vol. 8 of *The North American Indians*, ed. Frederick W. Hodge. 20 vols. Norwood, Mass.: Plimpton Press. Reprinted, New York: Johnson, 1970.   (83)

[56] ———. 1911. *The Yakima. The Klickitat. Salishan Tribes of the Interior. The Kutenai.* Vol. 7 of *The North American Indians: Being a Series of Volumes Picturing and Describing the Indians of the United States, the Dominion of Canada, and Alaska*, ed. Frederick W. Hodge. 20 vols. Norwood, Mass.: Plimpton Press. Reprinted, New York: Johnson, 1970. (38, 80ff.)

[57] Daughtery, Richard D. 1956. "Archaeology of the Lind Coulee Site, Washington." *Proceedings of the American Philosophical Society* 100:223–78.   (15)

[58] ———. 1956. *Early Man in the Columbia Intermontane Province.* University of Utah Anthropological Papers, no. 24.

Salt Lake City: University of Utah
Press. (13, 14)

[59] ———. 1962. "The Intermontane
Western Tradition." *American Antiquity*
28:144–50. (15)

*[60] ———. 1973. *The Yakima People*.
Phoenix· Indian Tribal Series. (79)

[61] De Smet, Jean Pierre, S.J. 1863. *New
Indian Sketches*. New York: D. and J.
Sadlier. New ed., New York: P. J.
Kenedy, Excelsior Catholic Publishing
House. Reprinted, Seattle: Shorey
Bookstore, 1971. (61)

[62] ———. 1905. *Life, Letters and Travels of
Father Pierre-Jean de Smet, S.J., 1801–
1873; Missionary Labors and Adventures
among the Wild Tribes of the North Ameri-
can Indians . . . Edited from the Original
Unpublished Manuscript Journals and Let-
ter Books and from His Printed Works, with
Historical, Geographical, Ethnological and
Other Notes; Also a Life of Father de Smet
. . . by Hiram Martin Chittenden and Alfred
Talbot Richardson*. 4 vols. New York: F.
P. Harper. (61, 65)

[63]   Desmond, Gerald R. 1952. *Gambling among the Yakima*. Catholic University Anthropological Series, no. 14. Washington, D.C.: Catholic University of American Press.   (64, 81, 83ff.)

[64]   Deutsch, Herman J. 1956. "Indian and White in the Inland Empire: The Conquest for the Land, 1880–1912." *Pacific Northwest Quarterly* 47:44–51.   (69)

[65]   Doty, James. 1855. "A True Copy of the Record of the Official Proceedings at the Council in the Walla Walla Valley, Held Jointly by Isaac L. Stevens Govn. & Supt. W. T. and Joel Palmer Supt. Ind. Affairs O.T. on the part of the United States with the Tribes of Indians Named in the Treaties Made at That Council June 9th and 11th, 1855." National Archives, Record Group 75. Washington, D.C.: Records of the Bureau of Indian Affairs. Available on microcopy T-494, roll 5, item 3.   (36)

[66]   ———. 1855–56. "Journal of Operations of Governor Isaac Ingalls Stevens, Superintendent of Indian Affairs and Commissioner, Treating with the Indian Tribes East of the Cascade Moun-

tains, in Washington Territory, and the Blackfeet and Neighboring Tribes, Near Great Falls of the Missourie, in the Year 1855; Including Therein Details of the Celebrated Indian Council at Walla Walla, and of the Blackfoot Council at Fort Benton, and the Commencement of the Indian Wars 1855–58." National Archives Record Group 75. Washington, D.C.: Records of the Bureau of Indian Affairs. Available on microcopy T-494, roll 5, item 9. Reprinted, Fairfield, Wash.: Ye Galleon Press, 1978. (35)

*[67]   Dryden, Cecil. 1968. *History of Washington*. Portland: Binfords and Mort. (58)

[68]   DuBois, Cora. 1938. *The Feather Cult of the Middle Columbia*. General Series in Anthropology 7. Menasha, Wis.: George Banta. (21, 91, 93)

[69]   Dunn, Jacob P. 1886. *Massacres of the Mountains: A History of the Indian Wars of the Far West, 1815–1875*. London: Eyre and Spottiswoode; New York: Harper and Brothers. Reprinted, 1963. (60)

[70]   Ekland, Roy E. 1969. "The 'Indian

Problem': Pacific Northwest, 1879."
Oregon Historical Quarterly 70:101–38.   (67)

[71]   Elliott, T. C. 1927. "Steptoe Butte and
Steptoe Battlefield." *Washington Historical Quarterly* 18:243–53.   (55)

[72]   ———. 1934. "The Murder of
Peu-Peu-Mox-Mox." *Oregon Historical
Quarterly* 35:123–30.   (45)

[73]   Ellis, Richard N., ed. 1972. *The Western
American Indian: Case Studies in Tribal
History*. Lincoln: University of Nebraska
Press. See [275].

[74]   Evans, Elwood. 1889. *History of the Pacific Northwest: Oregon and Washington*. 2
vols. Portland: North Pacific History
Company.   (74)

[75]   Ewers, John C. 1955. *The Horse in
Blackfoot Indian Culture: With Comparative Material from Other Western Tribes*.
Bureau of American Ethnology Bulletin 159. Washington, D.C.: Government
Printing Office. Reprinted, Smithsonian Institution Press, 1980.   (19)

[76]   Ferrand, Livingston. 1917. "Sahaptin

Tales." *Memoirs of the American Folk-Lore Society* 11:135–79. See [22].   (93)

[77] Filloon, Ray M. 1952. "Huckleberry Pilgrimage." *Pacific Discovery* 5(3):4–13.(86, 90)

[78] Fitch, James B. 1974. "Economic Development in a Minority Enclave: The Case of the Yakima Nation, Washington." Ph.D. diss., Stanford University.   (72)

[79] Fitzpatrick, Darleen Ann. 1968. "The 'Shake': The Indian Shaker Curing Ritual among the Yakima." Master's thesis, University of Washington.   (93)

[80] Franchère, Gabriel. 1820. *Relation d'un voyage à la côte du Nord-ouest de l'Amérique Septentrionale, dans les années 1810, 11, 12, 13 et 14.* Montreal: Impr. de C. B. Pasteur. New ed., trans. and ed. J. V. Huntington, *Narrative of a Voyage to the Northwest Coast of America in the Years 1811, 1812, 1813, and 1814; or, The First American Settlement on the Pacific.* New York: Redfield, 1854. Reprinted in *Early Western Travels, 1748–1846,* ed. Reuben Gold Thwaites, 32 vols. Cleveland: Arthur H. Clark, 1904–7. See 6:167–410.   (24)

[81]   French, David. 1961. "The Wishram-
       Wasco." In *Perspectives in American In-
       dian Culture Change*, ed. Edward H.
       Spicer, pp. 340–430. Chicago: Univer-
       sity of Chicago Press.   (100)

[82]   French, Katherine S. 1955. "Culture
       Segments and Variation in Contempo-
       rary Social Ceremonialism on the Warm
       Springs Reservation, Oregon." Ph.D.
       diss., Columbia University.   (100)

[83]   Fryxell, R., et al. 1968. "Human Re-
       mains of Mid-Pinedale Age from
       Southeastern Washington." *American
       Antiquity* 33:511–15.   (13)

[84]   Fuller, George W. 1928. *The Inland
       Empire of the Pacific Northwest: A History*.
       3 vols. Spokane: H. G. Linderman.   (75)

*[85] ———. 1931. *A History of the Pacific
       Northwest*. New York: Alfred A. Knopf.
       Rev. ed., 1949.   (67, 75, 92)

[86]   Gairdner, Dr. 1841. "Notes on the Ge-
       ography of the Columbia River." *Jour-
       nal of the Royal Geographical Society of
       London* 11:250–57.   (90)

[87]   Garrand, Victor, S.J. 1977. *Augustine Laure, S.J., Missionary to the Yakimas*, ed. Edward J. Kowrach. Fairfield, Wash.: Ye Galleon Press.   (71)

[88]   Garrecht, Francis A. 1928. "An Indian Chief." *Washington Historical Quarterly* 19:165–80.   (70)

[89]   Garretson, Margaret Ann. 1968. "The Yakima Indians, 1855–1935: Background and Analysis of the Rejection of the Indian Reorganization Act." Master's thesis, University of Washington.   (71)

[90]   Gates, Charles M., ed. 1940. *Messages of the Governors of the Territory of Washington to the Legislative Assembly, 1854–1889*. Seattle: University of Washington Press.(39, 51)

[91]   ———., ed. 1941. *Readings in Pacific Northwest History: Washington, 1790–1895*. Seattle: University Bookstore.   (46)

[92]   Gibbs, George. 1855. "Report of Mr. George Gibbs to Captain McClellan on the Indian Tribes of the Territory of Washington," dated 4 March 1854; and "Report of George Gibbs upon the Geology of the Central Portion of

Washington Territory," dated 1 May
1854. In *Reports of Explorations and Surveys to Ascertain the Most Practicable and Economical Route for a Railroad from the Mississippi River to the Pacific Ocean*, ed.
Isaac Ingalls Stevens, 1:402–34,
1:473–86. 33d Congr., 2d sess. Senate
Executive Document no. 78. Washington, A. O. P. Nicholson. Reprinted as
George Gibbs, *Indian Tribes of Washington Territory*, Fairfield, Wash.: Ye Galleon Press, 1978.   (19, 20, 21, 32, 82ff.)

[93]   ———. 1857. "Letter to James G.
Swan," dated 7 January 1857. In *The Northwest Coast; or, Three Years' Residence in Washington Territory*, ed. James G.
Swan, pp. 426–29. New York: Harper
and Brothers. Reprinted, Seattle, University of Washington Press, 1972.   (32)

*[94]   Glauert, Earl T., and Merle H. Kunz,
eds. 1972. *The Kittitas Indians*. Ellensburg, Wash.: Ellensburg Public Library.   (28, 37)

*[95]   ———. 1976. *Kittitas Frontiersmen*. Ellensburg, Wash.: Ellensburg Public Library.   (32, 44)

[96] Gogol, J. M. 1979. "Columbia River Indian Basketry." *American Indian Basketry Magazine* 1(1):4–9. (87)

[97] ———. 1980. "Cornhusk Bags and Hats of the Columbia Plateau Indians." *American Indian Basketry Magazine* 1(2):4–11. (88)

[98] Gosnell, W. B. 1926. "Indian War in Washington Territory—Report of Special Agent W. B. Gosnell." *Washington Historical Quarterly* 17:289–99. (52)

[99] Griswold, Gillett G. 1954. "Aboriginal Patterns of Trade between the Columbia Basin and the Northern Plains." Master's thesis, University of Montana.(20, 85)

[100] ———. 1970. "Aboriginal Patterns of Trade between the Columbia Basin and the Northern Plains." *Archaeology in Montana* 11:1–96. (19, 20, 85)

*[101] Guie, H. Dean. 1937. *Tribal Days of the Yakimas*. Yakima, Wash.: Republic Publishing Company. (19, 21, 81, 90)

*[102] ———. 1956. *Bugles in the Valley: Garnett's Fort Simcoe*. Yakima, Wash.: Re-

public Press. Rev. ed., Portland: Oregon Historical Society, 1977.   (48)

[103]   Gunther, Erna. 1950. "The Westward Movement of Some Plains Traits." *American Anthropologist,* n.s., 52:174–80.   (19)

[104]   Haeberlin, H. K., James A. Teit, and Helen H. Roberts. 1928. "Coiled Basketry in British Columbia and Surrounding Region." In *Forty-first Annual Report of the Bureau of American Ethnology,* pp. 119–484. Washington, D.C.; Government Printing Office.   (87)

*[105]   Haines, Francis. 1955. *The Nez Perces.* Norman: University of Oklahoma Press.   (18, 100)

[106]   Hale, Horatio. 1846. *Ethnography and Philology.* Philadelphia: Printed by C. Sherman. Vol. 6 of Wilkes [276]. (2, 27, 86, 95)

[107]   Haller, Granville O. n.d. "The Indian War of 1855–6 in Washington and Oregon." In manuscript collections, documents section, University of Washington Library, Seattle. Haller box 2, folder 5.   (41, 52)

[108] ———. n.d. "Kamiarkin—In History: Memoir of the War, in the Yakima Valley, 1855–1856." Pacific Manuscript A128. H. H. Bancroft Collection, Bancroft Library, University of California, Berkeley. Available in University of Washington Library, Seattle, and Kamiakin Research Institute, Yakima Indian Nation, Toppenish, Wash.   (41, 52)

[109] ———. 1863. "The Dismissal of Major Granville O. Haller of the Regular Army, of the United States, by Order of the Secretary of War, in Special Orders No. 331, of July 25, 1863"; "A Brief Memoir of His Military Services, and a Few Observations." Paterson, N.J.: Daily Guardian Office.   (41, 44, 52)

[110] Harmon, Ray. 1971. "Indian Shaker Church: The Dalles." *Oregon Historical Quarterly* 72:148–58.   (93)

[111] Harrington, M. R. 1921. "Some String Records of the Yakima." *Indian Notes and Monographs* 16:48–64. (Museum of American Indian, Heye Foundation.)   (87)

*[112] Helland, Maurice. 1975. *They Knew Our Valley*. Yakima, Wash.: Printed by the author.   (76, 89)

[113] Hembree, Waman C. 1925. "Yakima Indian War Diary." *Washington Historical Quarterly* 16(4):273–83.   (51)

[114] Hodge, Frederick Webb., ed. 1907, 1910. *Handbook of American Indians North of Mexico*. 2 vols. Bureau of American Ethnology Bulletin 30. Washington, D.C.: Government Printing Office. Reprinted, New York: Pageant Books, 1959; Totowa, N.J.: Rowan and Littlefield, 1975.   (80)

[115] Howard, Oliver O. 1907. *My Life and Experiences among Our Hostile Indians*. Hartford, Conn.: A. D. Worthington.   (67, 92)

[116] Huggins, E. L. 1891. "Smohalla, the Prophet of Priest Rapids." *Overland Monthly* 17:208–15.   (92)

[117] Hulse, Frederick S. 1957. "Linguistic Barriers to Gene-Flow: The Blood Groups of the Yakima, Okanagon, and Swinomish Indians." *American Journal of Physical Anthropology* 15(2):235–46.   (96)

[118] Irving, Washington. 1850. *The Adventures of Capt. Bonneville, U.S.A. in the Rocky Mountains and the Far West*. New

York: G. P. Putnam. Reprinted, New
York: Twayne, 1977. (27, 90)

[119] Jacobs, Melville. 1929. "Northwest
Sahaptin Texts, Part I." *University of
Washington Publications in Anthropology*
2:175–244. (94)

[120] ———. 1931. "A Sketch of Northern
Sahaptin Grammar." *University of Washington Publications in Anthropology*
4:85–292. (96, 98)

[121] ———. 1932. "Sahaptin Kinship
Terms." *American Anthropologist*, n.s.,
34:688–93. (96)

[122] ———. 1934. *Northwest Sahaptin Texts,
Part 1*. Columbia University Contribu-
tions to Anthropology 19. New York:
Columbia University Press. (94)

[123] ———. 1937. "Historic Perspectives in
Indian Languages of Oregon and
Washington." *Pacific Northwest Quarterly*
28:55–74. (96, 98)

[124] ———. 1937. *Northwest Sahaptin Texts,
Part 2*. Columbia University Contribu-
tions to Anthropology 19. New York:
Columbia University Press. (94)

[125] Johansen, Dorothy O., and Charles M. Gates. 1957. *Empire of the Columbia: A History of the Pacific Northwest.* New York: Harper. (75)

[126] Josephy, Alvin M., Jr. 1965. *The Nez Perce Indians and the Opening of the Northwest.* New Haven: Yale University Press. Reprinted, abridged ed., 1971. (38, 100)

[127] Kane, Paul. 1859. *Wanderings of an Artist among the Indians of North America from Canada to Vancouver's Island and Oregon through the Hudson's Bay Companies Territory and Back Again.* London: Longman, Brown, Green, and Roberts. New ed., J. Russell Harper, ed., *Paul Kane's Frontier, Including "Wanderings of an Artist among the Indians of North America" by Paul Kane.* Austin: University of Texas Press, 1971. (28, 86, 98)

[128] Kappler, Charles J., comp. 1903–41. *Indian Affairs: Laws and Treaties.* 5 vols. Washington, D.C.: Government Printing Office. Vol. 2. *Treaties*, 1904. Senate Doc. no. 452, 57th Cong., 1st sess., serial no. 4254. Reprinted, New York: Interland, 1972. (39)

[129] Kelly, Plympton J. 1976. *We Were Not Summer Soldiers: The Indian War Diary of Plympton J. Kelly, 1855–1856.* Introduction and annotations by William N. Bischoff, S.J. Tacoma: Washington State Historical Society.   (45, 47, 51)

[130] Keyes, Erasmus D. 1884. *Fifty Years' Observation of Men and Events, Civil and Military.* New York: C. Scribner's Sons.(56, 57)

[131] Kip, Lawrence. 1855. *The Indian Council in the Valley of the Walla Walla, 1855.* San Francisco: Whitton, Towne. Reprinted in *Sources of the History of Oregon*, ed. F. G. Young. Contributions of the Department of Economics and History, University of Oregon. Eugene: Star Job Office.   (36)

[132] ———. 1859. *Army Life on the Pacific: A Journal of the Expedition against the Northern Indians, the Tribes of the Coeur d'Alenes, Spokanes, and Pelouzes in the Summer of 1858.* New York: Redfield.   (56)

*[133] Kirk, Ruth, and Richard D. Daugherty. 1978. *Exploring Washington Archaeology.* Seattle: University of Washington Press.   (12)

[134]   Krause, Marilyn L. 1969. "A Study of
        Drinking on a Plateau Indian Reserva-
        tion." Master's thesis, University of
        Washington, Seattle.   (72)

[135]   Krieger, Herbert W. 1928. "A Prehis-
        toric Pit House Village Site on the Co-
        lumbia River at Wahluke, Grant
        County, Washington." *Proceedings of the
        United States National Museum* 73:1–29.   (14)

[136]   Kuykendall, George B. 1889. "The In-
        dians of the Pacific Northwest." In *His-
        tory of the Pacific Northwest: Oregon and
        Washington*, ed. Elwood Evans, 2:60–95.
        Portland: Northern Pacific History
        Company.   (81, 93)

[137]   Leechman, J. D. 1921. "String Records
        of the Northwest." *Indian Notes and
        Monographs* 16:1–47. (New York,
        Museum of the American Indian, Heye
        Foundation.)   (87)

[138]   Leonhardy, Frank C., and David G.
        Rice. 1970. "A Proposed Culture
        Typology for the Lower Snake River
        Region, Southeastern Washington."
        Northwest Anthropological Research Notes
        4:1–29.   (15)

[139] Lewis, Albert B. 1906. "Tribes of the Columbia Valley and the Coast of Washington and Oregon." *Memoirs of the American Anthropological Association* 1:147–209. Reprinted, Millwood, N.Y.: Kraus, 1964. (80)

[140] Lewis, Meriwether, William Clark, et al. 1904–5. *Original Journals of the Lewis and Clark Expedition, 1804–1806; Printed from the Original Manuscripts . . . , Including Note-Books, Letters, Maps, Etc., and the Journals of Charles Floyd and Joseph Whitehouse, Now for the First Time Published in Full and Exactly as Written*, ed. Reuben Gold Thwaites. 8 vols. New York: Dodd, Mead. Reprinted, New York: Antiquarian Press, 1959; New York: Arno, 1969. (2, 5, 12, 20ff.)

[141] Lewis, William S. 1920. "The First Militia Companies in Eastern Washington Territory." *Washington Historical Quarterly* 11(4):243–49. (42)

[142] Lobb, Allan. 1978. *Indian Baskets of the Northwest Coast*. Portland: Graphic Arts Center. (88)

[143] Lockley, Fred. 1928. *History of the Co-*

lumbia River Valley from the Dalles to the Sea. 3 vols. Chicago: S. J. Clarke. (67, 75, 81)

[144] Longmire, David. 1917. "First Immigrants to Cross the Cascades." *Washington Historical Quarterly* 8:22–28.   (30)

[145] ———. 1932. "Narrative of James Longmire, a Pioneer of 1853." *Washington Historical Quarterly* 23:47–60, 138–50.   (30)

[146] Lyman, W. D. 1919. *History of the Yakima Valley, Washington, Comprising Yakima, Kittitas and Benton Counties.* Chicago: S. J. Clarke.   (2, 74)

[147] McClellan, George B. 1853. "Journal, May 20–December 15, 1853." Manuscript Division, Library of Congress, Washington, D.C. Available as microfilm A228, University of Washington Library, Seattle.   (31)

[148] ———. 1855. "General Reports of the Survey of the Cascades, Feb. 25, 1853." 33d Congress. 2d sess. House Exec. Doc. no. 91, Serial 791, pp. 188–201. Washington: A. O. P. Nicholson.   (32)

[149] McDonald, Angus. 1917. "Angus McDonald: A Few Items of the West." Edited by F. W. Howay, William S. Lewis, and Jacob A. Meyers. *Washington Historical Quarterly* 8:188–229. (25, 26, 32)

[150] McLoughlin, John. 1948. *Letters of Dr. John McLoughlin Written at Fort Vancouver, 1829–1832.* Edited by Burt Brown Barker. Portland: Binsfords and Mort. (21, 25, 26)

[151] MacMurray, J. W. 1884. "Reports of August 26th and September 19th, 1884, to the Acting Assistant Adjutant General, Department of the Columbia." National Archives Record Group 94. Washington, D.C.: United States National Archives. (65, 89)

[152] ———. 1887. "The 'Dreamers' of the Columbia River Valley in Washington Territory." *Transactions of the Albany Institute* 11:241–48. (65, 77, 89, 90)

[153] McWhorter, Lucullus V. 1913. *The Crime against the Yakimas*. North Yakima, Wash.: Republic Printers. Reprinted, Seattle: Shorey Book Store, 1965. (69, 70, 87)

[154]   ———.1916. "The Continued Crime
against the Yakimas." *American Patriot.*   (69)

[155]   ———. 1920. *The Discards: By He-Mene
Ka-Wan, "Old Wolf."* Printed by the
author.   (69)

*[156]   ———. 1937. *Tragedy of Wahk-Shum:
Prelude to the Yakima Indian War, 1855–
1856.* North Yakima, Wash.: Republic
Printers. Reprinted, Fairfield, Wash.:
Ye Galleon Press, 1968.   (37, 41, 42, 53)

*[157]   ———. 1952. *Hear Me, My Chiefs! Nez
Perce History and Legend.* Caldwell,
Idaho: Caxton Printers.   (38)

*[158]   Manring, Benjamin Franklin. 1912.
*Conquest of the Coeur d'Alenes, Spokanes,
and Palouses.* Spokane: Inland Printing
Company. Reprinted, Fairfield, Wash.:
Ye Galleon Press, 1975.   (57)

[159]   Mason, Otis Tufton. 1904. "Aboriginal
American Indian Basketry: Studies in a
Textile Art without Machinery." *Annual
Report, United States National Museum for
1902–1904*, pp. 171–548. Reprinted,
Santa Barbara: Peregrine Smith, 1976.   (87)

[160] Masterson, James R. 1946. "The Records of the Washington Superintendency of Indian Affairs, 1853–1874." *Pacific Northwest Quarterly* 37:31–57. (63)

[161] Meinig, D. W. 1968. *The Great Columbia Plain: A Historical Geography, 1805–1910*. Seattle: University of Washington Press. (18, 38, 64, 75, 98)

[162] Merk, Frederick, ed. 1931. *Fur Trade and Empire: George Simpson's Journal, 1824–1825*. Cambridge: Harvard University Press. See [216]. (86)

[163] Mooney, James. 1896. *The Ghost-Dance Religion and the Sioux Outbreak of 1890*. 14th Annual Report of the Bureau of Ethnology. Washington, D.C.: Government Printing Office. Reprinted, Chicago: University of Chicago Press, 1965. (66, 77, 90, 92)

[164] ———. 1928. "The Aboriginal Population of America North of Mexico." *Smithsonian Miscellaneous Collections* 80(7):1–40. (21, 22)

[165] Mullan, John. 1859. "Topographical Memoir of Col. George Wright's Cam-

paign against the Hostile Indians in Oregon and Washington Territories." 35th Congress, 2d sess., Senate Exec. Doc. no. 32, serial set 984, pp. 1–82.   (56)

[166] Murdock, George P., and Timothy J. O'Leary. 1975. *Ethnographic Bibliography of North America*. 5 vols. 4th ed. New Haven: Human Relations Area Files Press.   (79)

[167] Nelson, Charles M. 1969. *The Sunset Creek Site (45-KT-28) and Its Place in Plateau Prehistory*. Washington State University Laboratory of Anthropology, Report of Investigations 47. Pullman: Washington State University.   (15)

[168] Nelson, Denys. 1928. "Yakima Days." *Washington Historical Quarterly* 19(1):45–51; 19(2):117–33; 19(3): 181–92.   (29, 43)

[169] Nesmith, J. W. 1976. "Letter to George C. Curry, Governor of Oregon, Nov. 19, 1855." In *Kittitas Frontiersmen*, ed. Earl T. Glauert and Merle H. Kunz, pp. 110–12. Ellensburg, Wash.: Ellensburg Public Library.   (44)

[170] Overmeyer, Philip H. 1941. "George B. McClellan and the Pacific Northwest." *Pacific Northwest Quarterly* 32:3–60.　　(32)

*[171] Pace, Robert E., comp. 1977. *The Land of the Yakimas*. Edited by the Kamiakin Research Institute. Toppenish, Wash.: Yakima Indian Nation Tribal Council. (72, 102)

[172] Painter, Robert M. 1924. "Journal, October, 1855–May, 1856." Edited by J. Orin Oliphant. *Washington Historical Quarterly* 15:13–26.　　(47, 51)

[173] Painter, William Charles. 1924. "Journal, October, 1855–January, 1856." Edited by J. Orin Oliphant. *Washington Historical Quarterly* 15:27–31.　　(47, 51)

[174] Palmer, Joel. 1856. "Letter Dated October 3, 1855, to J. Cain, Acting Supt. of Indian Affairs, Washington." 34th Congr., 1st sess. House Exec. Doc. no. 93. Serial set 858. Washington, D.C.: Cornelius Wendell, Printer.　　(12)

[175] Pambrun, Andrew D. 1979. *Sixty Years on the Frontier in the Pacific Northwest*. Edited from original manuscripts by Edward J. Kowrach. Fairfield, Wash.: Ye Galleon Press.　　(37)

[176]   Pandosy, Marie Charles. 1862. *Grammar and Dictionary of the Yakima Language.* Translated from French by George Gibbs and J. G. Shea. New York: Cramoisy Press. Reprinted, New York: AMS Press.   (29, 95)

[177]   Parker, Samuel. 1838. *Journal of an Exploring Tour beyond the Rocky Mountains, under the Direction of the American Board of Commissioners for Foreign Missions in the Years 1835, 1836 and 1837.* Ithaca, N.Y.: Published by the author. Reprinted, Minneapolis: Ross and Haines, 1967.   (2, 28, 90)

[178]   Peltier, Jerome, and B. C. Payette. 1972. *Warbonnets and Epaulets: With Pre and Post Factors, Documented, of the Steptoe-Wright Indian Campaigns of 1858 in Washington Territory.* Montreal: Payette Radio.   (51, 58)

[179]   Prosch, Thomas W. 1915. "The Indian War in Washington Territory." *Oregon Historical Quarterly* 16:1–23.   (55, 60)

[180]   *Puget Sound Courier.* 1855. Articles from 5, 12 July 1855. (Steilacoom, Wash.)   (40)

[181] Ray, Verne F. 1932. *The Sanpoil and Nespelem: Salishan Peoples of Northeastern Washington.* University of Washington Publications in Anthropology 5. Seattle: University of Washington Press. (99)

[182] ———. 1936. "Native Villages and Groupings of the Columbia Basin." *Pacific Northwest Quarterly* 27:99–152. (86, 98)

[183] ———. 1939. *Cultural Relations in the Plateau of Northwestern America.* Publications of the Frederick Webb Hodge Anniversary Publication Fund 3. Los Angeles: Southwest Museum. (20, 85, 86)

[184] Ray, Verne F., et al. 1938. "Tribal Distribution in Eastern Oregon and Adjacent Regions." *American Anthropologist,* n.s., 40:384–415. (83, 98)

[185] Reese, J. W. 1965. "OMV's Fort Henrietta: On Winter Duty, 1855–56." *Oregon Historical Quarterly* 66:132–60. (45)

*[186] Relander, Click. 1956. *Drummers and Dreamers.* Caldwell, Idaho: Caxton Printers. (77, 92, 100)

*[187] ———. 1962. *Strangers on the Land.* Yakima, Wash.: Franklin Press. (63, 68, 69, 102)

[188]   Rice, David G. 1972 *The Windust Phase in Lower Snake River Region Prehistory.* Laboratory of Anthropology Reports of Investigations 50. Pullman: Washington State University.   (13)

[189]   Richards, Kent. D. 1972. "Isaac I. Stevens and Federal Military Power in Washington Territory." *Pacific Northwest Quarterly* 63:81–86.   (34)

[190]   ———. 1979. *Isaac I. Stevens: Young Man in a Hurry.* Provo, Utah: Brigham Young University Press.   (35)

[191]   Rigsby, Bruce J. 1965. "Continuity and Change in Sahaptin Vowel Systems." *International Journal of American Linguistics* 31(4):306–11.   (97)

[192]   ———. 1965. "Linguistic Relations in the Southern Plateau." Ph.D. diss., University of Oregon.   (97)

[193]   Robie, A. B. 1858. "Report of Special Agent A. H. Robie to the Commissioner of Indian Affairs, July 31, 1857." 35th Cong., 1st Sess. House Exec. Doc. no. 2. Serial 942. Washington, D.C.: James B. Steedman.   (21, 82)

*[194] Roe, Frank G. 1955. *The Indian and the Horse*. Norman: University of Oklahoma Press. (18)

[195] Ross, Alexander. 1849. *Adventures of the First Settlers on the Oregon or Columbia River*. London: Smith, Elder. See [249]. (2, 18, 20, 24, 83, 86)

*[196] ———. 1855. *The Fur Hunters of the Far West: A Narrative of Adventures in the Oregon and Rocky Mountains. . . .* 2 vols. London: Smith, Elder. Reprinted, Norman: University of Oklahoma Press, 1956. (24, 25, 84)

[197] Roy, Prodipto. 1961. *The Socio-Economic Status of the Yakima Nation*. Institute of Agricultural Sciences Circular 397. Pullman: Washington State University. (71)

[198] Royce, Charles C., comp. 1899. *Indian Land Cessions in the United States*. Part 2 of *Eighteenth Annual Report of the Bureau of American Ethnology*. Washington, D.C.: Government Printing Office. Reprinted, New York: Arno, 1971; New York: AMS, 1973. (39)

[199] Ruby, Robert H. 1966. "A Healing Service in the Shaker Church." *Oregon Historical Quarterly* 67:347–55. (93)

*[200]   Ruby, Robert H., and John A. Brown. 1965. *Half-Sun on the Columbia*. Norman: University of Oklahoma Press.   (67, 99)

*[201]   ———. 1972. *The Cayuse Indians: Imperial Tribesmen of Old Oregon*. Norman: University of Oklahoma Press.   (99)

[202]   Russell, Pearl. 1919. "Analysis of the Pacific Railroad Reports." *Washington Historical Quarterly* 10:3–16.   (33)

[203]   Sahaptin River Tribes Consortium. 1976. *Sahaptin River Tribes: Language Project*. n.p.: Sahaptin River Tribes Consortium.   (97)

[204]   St. Onge, Louis Napoléon. 1872. *Alphabet Yakama contenant Les prières, les cantiques et le catéchisme dans la même langue*. Montreal: Imprime à la Providence.   (29, 95)

[205]   Santee, J. F. 1933. "Pio-Pio-Mox-Mox." *Oregon Historical Quarterly* 34:164–76.   (45)

[206]   Schlick, Mary D. 1979. "A Columbia River Indian Basket Collected by Lewis and Clark in 1805." *American Indian Basketry Magazine* 1(1):10–13.   (87)

[207]   ———. 1980. "Art Treasures of the Columbia Plateau." *American Indian Basketry Magazine* 1(2):12–21.   (88)

[208]   Schoolcraft, Henry Rowe. 1851–57.
*Historical and Statistical Information Re-
specting the History, Conditions, and Pros-
pects of the Indian Tribes of the United
States.* 6 vols. Philadelphia: Lippincott,
Grambo. Index compiled by Francis S.
Nichols. Washington, D.C.: Govern-
ment Printing Office, 1954. Reprinted
in 7 vols., including index, New York:
AMS, 1969.   (80)

[209]   Schuster, Helen H. 1975. *Yakima Indian
Traditionalism: A Study in Continuity and
Change.* Ph.D. diss., University of Washington. Ann Arbor: University Micro-
films.   (81, 86, 89, 91)

[210]   ———. 1978. "Children's Drawings
and Perceptions of 'Indianness.'"*Ethos*
6(3):159–74.   (72)

[211]   Sebring, F. M. 1928. "The Indian Raid
on the Cascades in March, 1856." *Washington Historical Quarterly* 19:99–107.   (47, 53)

[212]   Seelatsee, Julia. 1967. "The Christmas

Festival among the Yakima." *Indian Historian* 1:8.   (90)

[213]   Seymour, Flora Warren. 1941. *Indian Agents of the Old Frontier*. New York: D. Appleton-Century.   (63)

[214]   Sheller, Roscoe. 1965. *The Name Was Olney*. Yakima, Wash.: Franklin Press. (45, 78)

[215]   Sheridan, Philip H. 1888. *Personal Memoirs of P. H. Sheridan, General, U.S. Army*. 2 vols. New York: Charles L. Webster.   (44, 47, 52)

[216]   Simpson, George. 1931. *Fur Trade and Empire: George Simpson's Journal, 1824–1825*. Edited by Frederick Merk. Cambridge: Harvard University Press.(25, 86)

[217]   Slickpoo, Allen P., Sr., and Deward E. Walker, Jr. 1973. *Noon Nee-Me-Poo (We, the Nez Perces): Culture and History of the Nez Perces*. Lapwai, Idaho: Nez Perce Tribe of Idaho.   (36, 101)

[218]   Smith, Harlan I. 1904. "A Costumed Human Figure from Tampico, Washington." *Bulletin of the American Museum of Natural History* 20:195–203.   (14)

[219] ———. 1910. *The Archaeology of the Yakima Valley*. Anthropological Papers 6. New York: American Museum of Natural History. (13)

[220] Smith, W. C. 1971. *Descriptive Archaeology of the Umtanum Creek Site (45-KT-101)*. Central Washington State College Occasional Papers 1. Ellensberg, Wash.: Central Washington State College, Department of Anthropology and Museum of Man. (15)

[221] Snowden, C. A. 1909–11. *History of Washington: The Rise and Progress of an American State*. 4 vols. New York: Century Company. (74)

[222] Spier, Leslie. 1935. *The Prophet Dance of the Northwest and Its Derivatives: The Source of the Ghost Dance*. General Series in Anthropology 1. Menasha, Wisc.: George Banta. (90)

[223] ———. 1936. *Tribal Distribution in Washington*. General Series in Anthropology 3. Menasha, Wisc.: George Banta. (83, 98)

[224] Spier, Leslie, and Edward Sapir. 1930. "Wishram Ethnography." *University of*

Washington Publications in Anthropology
3(3):151–300.   (99)

*[255] Splawn, Andrew J. 1917. *Ka-Mi-Akin, the Last Hero of the Yakimas*. Portland: Kilham Stationery and Printing Company. Reprinted, Yakima, Wash.: Caxton Printers, 1958.   (21, 38, 42, 53ff.)

[226] Sprague, Roderick. 1973. "The Pacific Northwest." In *The Development of North American Archaeology: Essays in the History of Regional Traditions*. ed. James E. Fitting. Garden City, N.Y.: Anchor Press.   (11)

[227] Stevens, Hazard. 1900. *The Life of Isaac Ingalls Stevens*. 2 vols. Boston and New York: Houghlin, Mifflin.   (34, 55)

[228] Stevens, Isaac Ingalls. 1855. "Report of Explorations for a Route for the Pacific Railroad, Near the 47th and 49th Parallels of North Latitude from St. Paul to Puget Sound." In *Reports of Explorations and Surveys to Ascertain the Most Practicable and Economical Route for a Railroad from the Mississippi River to the Pacific Ocean*. 12 vols. 33d Congr., 2d Sess. Senate Exec. Doc. no. 78, 1:1–651. Washington, D.C.: A. O. P. Nicholson.   (33)

[229] Stevens, Isaac Ingalls, et al. 1855–60. *Reports of Explorations and Surveys to Ascertain the Most Practicable and Economical Route for a Railroad from the Mississippi River to the Pacific Ocean.* 12 vols. Commonly referred to as *Pacific Railroad Reports.* Washington, D.C.: various printers for the U.S. Congress. See [228, 232]. (32)

[230] Stevens, Isaac Ingalls. 1855–56. "Letter to George W. Manypenny, Commissioner of Indian Affairs, December 22, 1855." 34th Congr., 1st Sess., House Exec. Doc. no. 93, Serial set 858. Washington: Cornelius Wendell. (45)

[231] ———. 1857. "Portion of the Map of the Indian Nations and Tribes of the Territory of Washington, etc., March 1857. Drawn by Wm. H. Carlton for Geo. W. Manypenny, Commissioner of Indian Affairs, April 30, 1857, Showing Ceded Portion of Yakima Nation Lands, Including Tabular Statement of Indian Population." Seattle: Neelans Litho. (39)

[232] ———. 1860. "Narrative and Final Report of Explorations for a Route for a

Pacific Railroad Near the 47th and 49th Parallels of North Latitude, from St. Paul to Puget Sound, 1855." In *Explorations and Surveys for a Railroad Route from the Mississippi River to the Pacific Ocean.* 12 vols. 36th Congress, 1st Sess. House Exec. Doc. no. 56, Washington, D.C.: Government Printing Office. See vol. 12.   (33)

[233]   ———. 1940. "Letters, 1857–1858." *Pacific Northwest Quarterly* 31:403–59.   (34)

[234]   Stewart, Edgar I., and Jane R. Stewart, eds. 1957. *The Columbia River.* Norman: University of Oklahoma Press. For original edition of Ross Cox see [48].   (25)

[235]   Strong, Emory. 1959. *Stone Age on the Columbia River.* Portland: Binsfords and Mort.   (16, 87)

[236]   Strong, James Clark, 1893. *Wah-Kee-Nah and Her People: The Curious Customs, Traditions and Legends of the North American Indian.* New York: G. P. Putnam's Sons.   (86)

[237]   Strong, William 1961 [1878]. "Knickerbocker Views of the Oregon Country:

Judge William Strong's Narrative." *Oregon Historical Quarterly* 62:57–87. (53)

[238] Strong, W. D., and W. E. Schenck. 1925. "Petroglyphs Near the Dalles of the Columbia River." *American Anthropologist,* n.s., 25:76–90. (16)

[239] Swanson, Earl H., Jr. 1962. *The Emergence of Plateau Culture.* Occasional Papers 8. Pocatello: Idaho State University Museum. (15)

[240] ———. 1970. "Sources for Plateau Prehistory." *American Antiquity* 35:495–96. (15)

[241] Swanson, Earl H., Jr., C. Melvin Aikens, David G. Rice, and Donald H. Mitchell. 1970. "Cultural Relations between the Plateau and Great Basin." *Northwest Anthropological Research Notes* 4:65–125. (101)

[242] Swanton, John Reed. 1952. *The Indian Tribes of North America.* Bureau of American Ethnology Bulletin 145. Washington, D.C.: Government Printing Office. (2, 80, 83)

[243] Symons, Thomas W. 1882. "Report of

an Examination of the Upper Columbia
River." 47th Congr., 1st sess. Senate
Exec. Doc. no. 186. Reprinted,
Fairfield, Wash.: Ye Galleon Press,
1967.   (66)

[244] Taylor, Herbert C., Jr., and Lester L.
Hoaglin, Jr. 1962. "The 'Intermittent
Fever' Epidemic of the 1830s on the
Lower Columbia River." *Ethnohistory*
9:160–78.   (22)

[245] Teit, James A. 1928. "The Middle Columbia Salish." *University of Washington
Publications in Anthropology* 2(4):83–128.   (21,
                                              22, 99)

[246] ———. 1930. "The Salishan Tribes of
the Western Plateaus." In *Forty-fifth Annual Report of the Bureau of American
Ethnology*, ed. Franz Boaz, pp. 23–396.
Washington, D.C.: Government Print-
ing Office.   (99)

[247] Thompson, Albert J. 1923. "Memories
of White Salmon and Its Pioneers."
Washington Historical Quarterly 14:108–
26.   (47, 53)

[248] Thompson, David. 1916. *David
Thompson's Narrative of His Explorations*

in Western America, 1784–1812. Edited by Joseph B. Tyrrell. Toronto: Champlain Society. New ed., ed. Richard Glover, Publications of the Champlain Society 40. Toronto: Champlain Society, 1962. (24, 83, 86, 87)

[249] Thwaites, Reuben Gold, ed. 1904–07. *Early Western Travels, 1748–1846: A Series of Annotated Reprints of Some of the Best and Rarest Contemporary Volumes of Travel, Descriptive of the Aborigines and Social and Economic Conditions in the Middle and Far West, during the Period of Early American Settlement.* 32 vols. Cleveland: Arthur H. Clark. See vols. 31–32 for index. Reprinted, New York: AMS, 1966. (25, 26)

[250] Townsend, John K. 1839. *Narrative of a Journey across the Rocky Mountains to the Columbia River, and a Visit to the Sandwich Islands, Chili.* . . . Philadelphia: Henry Perkins. Reprinted in Thwaites, ed., *Early Western Travels*, 21:107–369. See [249]. (26, 83, 90)

*[251] Travis, Helga Anderson. 1953. *Mool Mool: The Story of Fort Simcoe.* Kennewick, Wash.: Menerden Press. (48)

[252]   Trimble, W. J. 1914. "American and British Treatment of the Indians in the Pacific Northwest." *Washington Historical Quarterly* 5:32–54.   (71)

[253]   United States Commissioner of Indian Affairs. 1856. "Indian Disturbances in Oregon and Washington." *Report of the Commissioner of Indian Affairs.* 34th Congr., 1st Sess. House Exec. Doc. no. 48, serial set 853.   (45)

[254]   United States, Department of Interior. 1854–56. Records of the Washington Superintendency of Indian Affairs, Middle and Central Districts. Records of the National Archives, no. 5, roll 20. (33, 48)

[255]   United States, Department of Interior, Bureau of Indian Affairs. 1971. *Yakima Indian Nation.* Toppenish, Wash.: Center for the Study of Migrant and Indian Education.   (102)

[256]   United States, Indian Claims Commission. 1974. "Commission Findings." In *Interior Salish and Eastern Washington Indians IV.* American Indian Ethnohistory Series, ed. David Agee Horr. New York: Garland.   (39, 72)

[257] ———. 1974. *Interior Salish and Eastern Washington Indians IV*. American Indian Ethnohistory Series, ed. David Agee Horr. New York: Garland. Includes articles on the Yakimas by Stuart A. Chalfant, Verne F. Ray, and Angelo Anastasio.   (39, 72, 98)

[258] United States, Message of the President. 1856. "Indian Hostilities in Oregon and Washington Territories." *Message of the President, from Records of the United States Army Command,* 8 July 1856. 34th Congr., 1st Sess. House Exec. Doc. no. 118, serial set 859. (47, 51, 52)

[259] ———. 1856. "Indian Hostilities in Oregon and Washington." *Message of the President, from the Report of the Secy. of War, Dated April 17, 1856*. 34th Congr. 1st Sess. House Exec. Doc. no. 93, serial set 858.   (52)

[260] United States, Secretary of War. 1856. "Report of the Secy. of War, from the Records of the United States Army Command." 34th Congr., 3d Sess. Senate Exec. Doc. no. 5, serial set 876. (47, 49, 52, 54)

[261] ———. 1856 "Indian Disturbances in the Territories of Washington and Ore-

gon." *Report of the Secy. of War.* 34th Congr., 1st Sess. Senate Exec. Doc. no. 66, serial set 822.   (46, 51, 52)

[262]   ———. 1857. "Indian Affairs in Washington and Oregon Territories." *Papers from the Secy. of War on Indian Affairs on the Pacific, Dated Feb. 16, 1857.* 34th Congr., 3d Sess. House Exec. Doc. no. 76, serial set 906.   (43, 52)

[263]   ———. 1858. Correspondence between the Late Secy. of War and General Wool." *Message from the President.* 35th Congress, 1st Sess. House Exec. Doc. no. 88, serial set 956.   (46, 52)

[264]   ———. 1859. "Affairs in the Department of the Pacific." *Report of the Secy. of War.* 35th Congr., 2d Sess. House Exec. Doc. no. 2, vol. 2, serial set 998.   (56)

[265]   ———. 1860. "Affairs in the Department of Oregon." *Report of the Secretary of War.* 36th Congr., 1st Sess. House Exec. Doc. Ser. set 1051 (Military 3:91–121). Reprinted in De Smet [62].   (61)

[266]   Vaughn, Thomas, ed. 1971. *Paul Kane, the Columbia Wanderer: Sketches, Paintings*

and Comment, 1846–1847. Portland: Oregon Historical Society. (98)

[267] Victor, Frances F. 1894. *The Early Indian Wars of Oregon.* Salem, Oreg.: Frank C. Baker. (38, 43, 55, 74)

[268] Walker, Deward E., Jr. 1968. *Conflict and Schism in Nez Perce Acculturation: A Study of Religion and Politics.* Pullman: Washington State University Press. (101)

[269] Warren, Claude N. 1968. *The View from Wenas: A Study in Plateau Prehistory.* Idaho State University Museum Occasional Papers 24. Pocatello: Idaho State University Museum. (14, 16)

[270] Warren, Claude N., Allan L. Bryan, and Donald R. Tuohy. 1963. "The Goldendale Site and Its Place in Plateau Prehistory." *Tebiwa* 6(1):1–20. (14)

[271] Warren, Esther. 1977. *The Columbia Gorge Story.* Dalles, Oreg.: Itemizer-Observer Press. (78)

[272] Washington Territory, Governor of. 1857. *Message of the Governor of Washington Territory; Also the Correspondence with*

*the Secretary of War, Major General Wool,
the Officers of the Regular Army and the
Volunteer Service of Washington Territory.*
Olympia, Wash.: Edward Furste.   (45, 46,
49,50)

[273] Weeks, Thelma E. 1968. *The Speech of
Indian Children: Paralinguistic and Regis-
tral Aspects of the Yakima Dialect.* Palo
Alto, Calif.: Center for Cross-Cultural
Research.   (97)

[274] Whitehouse, Joseph. 1905. "Journal."
In *Original Journals of the Lewis and Clark
Expedition, 1804–1806*, ed. Reuben G.
Thwaites, vol. 7. See [249].   (20)

[275] Whitner, Robert Lee. 1959. "Grant's
Indian Peace Policy on the Yakima Res-
ervation, 1870–1882." *Pacific Northwest
Quarterly* 50:135–43. Reprinted in *The
Western American Indian: Case Studies in
Tribal History*, ed. Richard Ellis, pp.
50–62. See [73].   (64)

[276] Wilkes, Charles. 1845. *Narrative of the
United States Exploring Expedition during
the Years 1838–1842.* 5 vols. Philadelphia: Lea and Banchard. Vol. 4 reprinted in *Readings in Pacific Northwest
History: Washington, 1790–1895*, ed.

Charles M. Gates. Seattle: University Bookstore. See [106] for addendum. (27, 86)

[277] Wilkes, George. 1845. *History of Oregon, Geographical, Geological, and Political.* New York: Colyer. Reprinted in *Washington Historical Quarterly* 4(1):60–80; 4(2):139–60; 4(3):207–24 [1913]. (21, 26)

[278] Williams, Christina MacDonald McKenzie. 1922. "Reminiscences." *Washington Historical Quarterly* 13:107–17. (52)

*[279] Winthrop, Theodore. 1862. *The Canoe and the Saddle.* New York: Dodd, Mead. Reprinted as *The Canoe and Saddle, or Klalam and Klickitat.* Portland: Franklin-Ward, 1913. (29, 30)

[280] Wood, C. E. S. 1969. "Private Journal, 1879." *Oregon Historical Quarterly* 70:139–70. (90)

[281] Work, John. 1912–15. "Journal of John Work, 1824–1826." Edited by T. C. Elliott. *Washington Historical Quarterly* 3:198–228; 5:83–115, 163–191, 258–87; 6:26–49. (25)

[282]   ———. 1920. "John Work's Journal of a Trip from Fort Colville to Fort Vancouver and Return in 1828." Edited by William S. Lewis and Jacob A. Meyers. *Washington Historical Quarterly* 11:104–14.   (25, 26)

[283]   Wright, George. 1857. "Camp on the Natchess River, Washington Territory, June 11, 1856." 34th Congr., 3d Sess. Senate Exec. Doc. no. 5, serial set 876.   (47)

[284]   ———. 1859. "Expedition against the Northern Indians." General Orders of 4 July 1858, *Report of the War Department, Department of the Pacific, for 1858–1859*, 2:330–416. 35th Congr., 2d Sess. House Exec. Doc no. 2, serial set 998.   (56)

[285]   Wyeth, Nathaniel Jarvis. 1853. "Indian Tribes of the South Pass of the Rocky Mountains. The Salt Lake Basin. . . ." In *Historical and Statistical Information Respecting the History, Conditions and Prospects of the Indian Tribes of the United States*. Collected and prepared by Henry Rowe Schoolcraft. Part 1, pp. 204–28. See [208].   (26)

[286] ———. 1899. "The Correspondence and Journals of Captain Nathaniel J. Wyeth, 1831–1836: A Record of Two Expeditions for the Occupation of the Oregon Country, with Maps, Introduction and Index. . . ." Edited by F. G. Young. In *Sources of the History of Oregon* 1 (parts 3–4). Eugene: University Press. See [292]. (26)

[287] Yakima Indian Agency. 1962. *A Primer of the Yakimas*. Toppenish, Wash.: Yakima Indian Agency. (102)

[288] ———. 1962. *Yakima Indian Reservation Redevelopment Area, Overall Economic Development Plan*. Toppenish, Wash.: Yakima Indian Agency. (71)

[289] Yakima Indian Nation. 1972. *Religious Ceremony Commemorating the Restoration of Mount Adams*. n.p.: Yakima Indian Nation. (72, 102)

[290] Yakima Indian Nation, Education Division and Fort Wright College. 1979. *Multi-Cultural Early Childhood Curriculum for the Yakima Indian Nation*. Toppenish, Wash.: Kamiakin Research Institute. (97)

*[291]   Yakima Tribal Council. 1955. *The
         Yakimas: Treaty Centennial, 1855–1955*.
         Yakima, Wash.: Republic Press. (42, 62, 63ff.)

[292]   Young, Frederick George, ed. 1897–99.
         Sources of the History of Oregon. Eugene:
         University Press. See [286].   (36)

The Newberry Library
Center for the History of the American Indian
Founding Director: D'Arcy McNickle
Director: Francis Jennings

Established in 1972 by the Newberry Library, in conjunction with the Committee on Institutional Cooperation of eleven midwestern universities, the Center makes the resources of one of America's foremost research libraries in the Humanities available to those interested in improving the quality and effectiveness of teaching American Indian history. The Newberry's collections include some 110,000 volumes on the history of the American Indian and offer specialized resources for studying historical aspects of Indian-White relations and Indian linguistics. The Center also assists Native Americans engaged in writing tribal histories and developing educational materials.

ADVISORY COMMITTEE

Chairman: Alfonso Ortiz
University of New Mexico

George Abrams
Seneca-Iroquois National Museum

Nancy O. Lurie
Milwaukee Public Museum

Robert K. Thomas
University of Arizona

Robert F. Berkhofer
University of Michigan

Cheryl Metoyer-Duran
*University of California,
Los Angeles*

Antoinette McNickle Vogel
Gaithersburg, Maryland

Robert V. Dumont, Jr.
Fort Peck Community College

Father Peter J. Powell
St. Augustine Indian Center

Dave Warren
*Institute of American Indian Arts
Santa Fe*

Raymond D. Fogelson
University of Chicago

Faith Smith
*Native American Educational
Services/Antioch College;
Chicago*

Wilcomb E. Washburn
Smithsonian Institution

William T. Hagan
*State University of New
York College, Fredonia*

Sol Tax
University of Chicago

James Welch
Missoula, Montana